Gee, Wiz!

← antenna for extra-terrestrial contact

THE LIZARD
(LIZ FOR SHORT)
THE WIZ'S REPTILE SIDEKICK. HE LIKES TO MAKE COLD-BLOODED COMMENTS.

← special computer compass wand

THE WIZARD (WIZ FOR S[...]
ALSO KNOWN AS PROFESSOR B[...]
LOT OF TRICKS, IF HE COULD O[...]
HE IS EXCITABLE, ENTHUSIASTIC, AND [...]

Gee, Wiz!

How to Mix Art and Science
or The Art of Thinking Scientifically

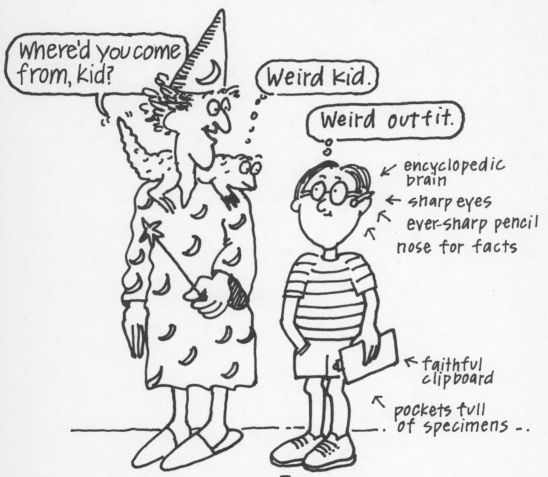

LINDA ALLISON AND DAVID KATZ
ILLUSTRATED BY LINDA ALLISON

a Brown Paper School book

**This book is dedicated to Galileo
and anybody else who believes that
the answers aren't all in books.**

This Brown Paper School book was edited and prepared
for publication at The Yolla Bolly Press, Covelo, California,
during the fall of 1982. The series is under the supervision of James
and Carolyn Robertson. Editorial and production staff: Dan
Hibshman, Diana Fairbanks, Joyca Cunnan, Barbara
Youngblood, and Juliana Yoder.

Second Printing

B

Library of Congress Cataloging in Publication Data

Allison, Linda.
Gee, Wiz!

(A Brown paper school book)
Summary: Presents projects to perform, using materials
commonly found around the house, that enable Smart Art
to present logical explanations for the magic and
mystery created by Gee Wiz.
1. Science—Experiments—Juvenile literature.
2. Scientific recreations—Juvenile literature.
[1. Science—Experiments. 2. Experiments. 3. Scientific
recreations] I. Katz, David, 1928-   . II. Title.
Q164.A4 1983   507'.8   83-9834
ISBN 0-316-03444-4
ISBN 0-316-03445-2 (pbk.)

BP hc
BB pb

First edition. Published simultaneously in Canada
by Little, Brown & Company (Canada) Limited.
Printed in the United States of America.

Introduction: science is an art

Some people think that science is test tubes, lab coats, smelly chemicals, or microscopes.

Science might use some of this equipment. But that's not science.

Science is a way of thinking about the world around you. It's a way of finding out what you don't know by figuring out what you do know. It's a way of getting answers to questions. Some people call it a method: the scientific method.

In the old days—before science—people got answers to their questions in other ways. They asked an expert. Or they checked in a book. Or they believed in magic.

A neat thing about science is that you don't need experts, books, or magical hocus-pocus to get answers.

Mostly what you need is a question and enough curiosity to find an answer.

Once you have a question, the next step in the scientific method is to make a guess about why the thing in question happens. A scientist calls this guess a *hypothesis* (hi *poth* a sis).

Next you, the scientist, need to test the guess. You think up an experiment that will tell you if the hypothesis is correct or not.

YOU CAN DO THIS EXPERIMENT WITH A GLASS OF LIGHT-COLORED SODA AND A FEW RAISINS.

While this experiment is being done, you watch and study what happens.

The next thing to do is to make up a theory that explains the results of the experiment. It should explain what is actually happening, which is not always what you hoped would happen. The theory may be the same as your original hypothesis, or it may be completely different. What's important is that it gets you farther along in answering your question.

How It Got to Be Science

In the old days the search for knowledge used to be one big subject called *philosophy* (fill *lahss* a fee). Philosophy is a Greek word that comes from *philos,* which means loved, and *sophia,* which means wisdom. A philosopher was a person who loved wisdom.

PUT THE RAISINS IN THE BOTTOM OF THE GLASS AND POUR IN THE SODA.

Later, philosophers divided themselves into two groups. There were philosophers who studied the nature of things. They were called natural philosophers. There were philosophers who studied the nature of the human soul. These were called moral philosophers. The general feeling was that the better class of philosophers looked into questions of the human soul, while the study of stars, insects, and forces were considered slightly second rate. This attitude stuck around for quite a few centuries. Natural philosophers finally got smart and realized this kind of attitude wasn't getting them anywhere. So they changed their name to scientists.

The word *science* comes from an old Latin word, *scientia,* which means knowledge. Since about 1700, scientists have been hard at work probing the secrets of the universe. They seem to be having more success than the moral philosophers, if you go by the numbers. Nowadays there are many more scientists than philosphers. Some scientists still think of themselves as natural philosophers, although most of them call themselves scientists.

Most likely they also call themselves some kind of ''ists,'' like physicists, botanists, chemists, or biologists, to name a few. ''Ist'' is a word ending that means one who specializes in something. The nature of science is proving to be so complicated (and fascinating) that its study is being divided up into smaller and smaller bits. It's sort of the ''divide and conquer'' approach.

1. HYPOTHESIZE (MAKE A THEORY) ABOUT WHAT'S HAPPENING.

Imagination

The projects in this book use a lot of different materials and supplies. We have tried to keep the equipment simple. Most of the projects require everyday things that you can find around the house. But sometimes, you won't have everything on the list.

How can you be a great scientist when you haven't got the right equipment? Don't panic.

Use your imagination. Put it to work. Find a substitute for that missing part. For instance, suppose you have everything ready to go for the project except for a paperclip. You could substitute wire, a twist tie, or a piece of tape instead. Scientists do that. They sometimes joke about their laboratories being held together with chewing gum and library glue.

Substitution won't work every time. Chemicals in the formulas aren't easily substituted. But a substitute will work a lot of the time. So when you're stuck, imagine. And remember, even if you had the world's fanciest equipment, the best artists and scientists would tell you that there's no substitute for imagination.

2. EXPERIMENT TO TEST YOUR HYPOTHESIS.

Science, Not to Be Trusted

You've seen the movies. You know what scientists are like. Some guy (they are always men in the movies) with thick glasses is fooling around in his lab. Sometimes he's a head-up-in-the-clouds scientist who is experimenting with something unfortunate, such as man-eating plants or radiation. More often, he's a power-crazed maniac who is tampering with the secret of life in order to control the world. Or his friends are evil guys wanting to rule the world. His experiments go wrong and create some runaway evil beast that can't be stopped—until the last five minutes of the film.

When people think of scientists they often think of those guys in the movies. They get nervous. Good grief, now what? they wonder. More atom bombs? More poisons? More monsters? They forget the beneficial discoveries made by scientists, such as computers that fit in your pocket, artificial hearts, and freeze-dried food.

I think I'm late for an appointment.

Now let's see what happens...

RAISINS IN BUBBLING SODA POP →

← RAISINS IN FLAT SODA POP

3. OBSERVE THE RESULTS OF THE EXPERIMENT.

The Answers

In this book, don't skip the questions. Try one or two on for size. Of course, most science books ask questions — usually a lot of them, all ganged up at the end of a chapter, waiting in ambush. They are often the simple type, like "Who is buried in Grant's Tomb?" Obvious. Or a question like "Prove the theory of relativity with a match book and a bowling ball." Impossible.

The last thing you need is a lot of questions like those. Not that this book doesn't ask questions. But in addition to questions it also gives you answers, in a section at the back. Now don't head there without a little bit of a struggle to answer questions on your own. Struggle will build up your brain and make it tougher — struggling is sort of like mental pushups.

The questions are ones you should be able to answer. They are meant to get you thinking about the way things work or to nudge you into putting together your own ideas into theories. Remember, having a question is the only way you can ever get to an answer. And for scientists, getting there is at least half the fun.

4. CONCLUSION: DOES THE EXPERIMENT PROVE THE THEORY? IF NOT, A NEW EXPERIMENT OR MAYBE A NEW THEORY IS NECESSARY.

Contents

Meniscus; Surface Tension; Brawny Bonds; Rearranging Molecules; Surface Swifties; Streaming Colors; Atomic Agitation; Diffusion; Molecular Motion

Small? Blowing Up Things; Magnifying Simply; Little Wonders; Magnifying History

Coming up next:

Exploding Colors:
the science of chromatography

Exploding Colors

Creeping Colors

They may look like ordinary felt tip markers, but some pens can explode into many colors. Not every color, just some. Half of the fun is trying to predict which colors.

The inks in marking pens are often combinations of several basic colored dyes. They are mixed together to make other colors.

Here is a method for testing whether or not your pens will explode into other colors and reveal their true identities.

You Will Need
absorbent paper, such as coffee filters, newsprint, or paper towels (the heavy-duty, commercial kind works best)
water-soluble colored markers
a glass
water

1. Cut the paper into 1-inch strips.
2. Fold a strip so that it touches the bottom of the glass and hangs over the edge.
3. Remove the paper and mark a crosswise stripe of color 2 inches from the bottom end.
4. Set the strip in a glass that has an inch of water in the bottom. The stripe will sit an inch above the water.
5. Watch the water as it crawls up the strip, and see if the color will break apart. If you're impatient, you might set up another test strip while you're waiting.

CHROMATOGRAPHY

2" { Mark the paper.

I predict green.

← Add water.

Wow! A color explosion!

Tape or hang the strips to dry.

16

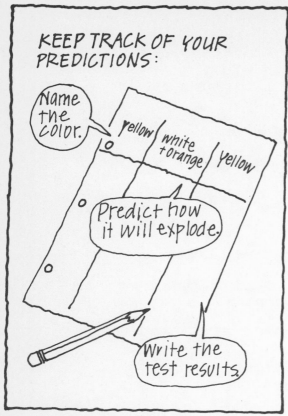

KEEP TRACK OF YOUR PREDICTIONS:

Name the color.

yellow | white + orange | yellow

Predict how it will explode.

Write the test results.

6. Before you test each color, be scientific and make a prediction about what colors will appear and crawl up the strip.

Base your guesses on your knowledge of which colors you need to mix to get other colors. Which color do you think contains the most other colors? Do you think you will find colors that refuse to explode?

Colorful History

Chromatography means color writing. The way substances crawl through paper, and the color patterns that result when they separate can be very useful to a scientist. Chromatography is a way that a chemist can test a liquid mixture, such as a drug or a dye, to find out what substances are in the mixture. The creepy pattern of colors left on the paper reveals this. The science of chromatography was invented in 1903 by a Russian botanist (plant scientist) named M.S. Tswett. He was studying the coloring materials that occur in plant life.

Chromatography: The Principle of the Thing

The colors of inks and dyes are molecules of coloring substances that are dissolved in a liquid base. When you write, the liquid part dries and leaves just the color behind. Some inks are a combination of coloring substances. These colors can be taken apart by adding either alcohol or water.

When the liquid in your experiment creeps up a test strip, it contacts the dried color. When it touches, it loosens up (dissolves) the coloring molecules in the ink and carries them up the strip. Different colors get carried along faster and farther than others, because some color molecules are bigger and heavier than others.

Actually, they explode in water.

Wet and Wild Colors

Can you imagine painting with a felt marker? It's not impossible, that is, if you know that pen inks will break apart into liquids again. Here is a way to get heavy-duty, deep dark lines and light colors all from the same felt marker. Meanwhile you can also test the pens for two kinds of solubility.

You Will Need
markers and ink pens, as many as you
  can find
rubbing alcohol, from the drugstore
water
glasses
two brushes

paper or absorbent towels (watercolor
paper works best)

1. Draw a line on a sheet of paper. Touch it at one end with a brush dipped in alcohol.

2. Touch it at the other end with a brush dipped in water.

The line will break apart and dissolve in one fluid or the other. If it is water, we describe it as water soluble. If it is alcohol, it is alcohol soluble.

To make a wet and wild artwork do the following:

1. Test all your pens to see what kinds of special effects you get with the solvents.

2. Draw something and go back and color it with the solvent brush.

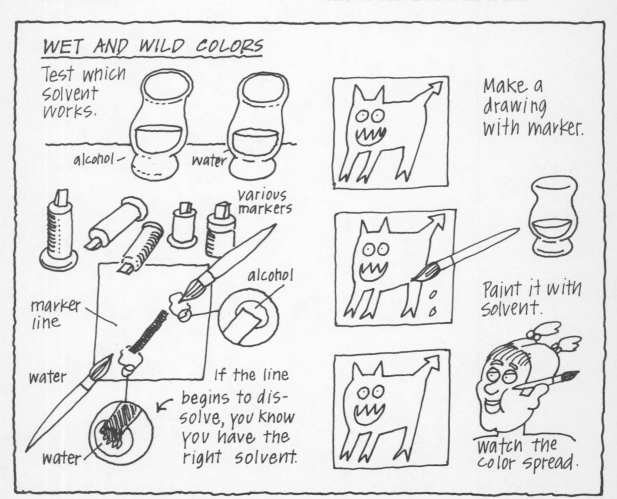

WET AND WILD COLORS

Test which solvent works.

alcohol — water

various markers

marker line

alcohol

water

If the line begins to dissolve, you know you have the right solvent.

water

Make a drawing with marker.

Paint it with solvent.

Watch the color spread.

18

WET AND WILD EFFECTS

Draw some lumps and bumps. Paint them with solvent. Lumps get soft and fuzzy.

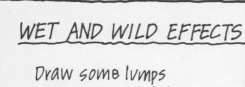

Wet lines to get a furry effect.

Touch up the outline when it dries.

WATER EFFECTS

Wet lines for rain.

Draw on wet paper for underwater effects.

Dissolve lines for a sky tone.

Dots for drips

SHADOW EFFECTS

Add solvent behind to make shadows.

Night-time effects

shadow alphabet.

Shadow eyes (top or bottom).

This is a really fun way to draw. You can get all sorts of interesting effects by letting two colors run together or by erasing part of a line (some inks will completely dissolve). Or by using a combination of two inks and only one solvent. Or by letting just part of your art go to pieces. Experiment with it.

Rainbow Pies

Creeping colors! It's rainbow pies. You can make beautiful colored designs by letting water do the work. All you need to do is a little planning. The absorbing action of water through the paper will spread, separate, and mix marker colors into round rainbow art.

You Will Need
round filter paper (circular coffee filters from the grocery store)
water soluble markers, food color, or dyes
water

1. Fold the filter paper into quarters.

2. Draw or drop a design on the paper.

3. Put the folded point into the water.

4. Wait while the water goes to work.

This will take a couple of hours.

While you're waiting here are some questions to think over:

Does time make any difference in the design you get? Can you create a green design without a green marker? Does the order of how you color the paper change the design results?

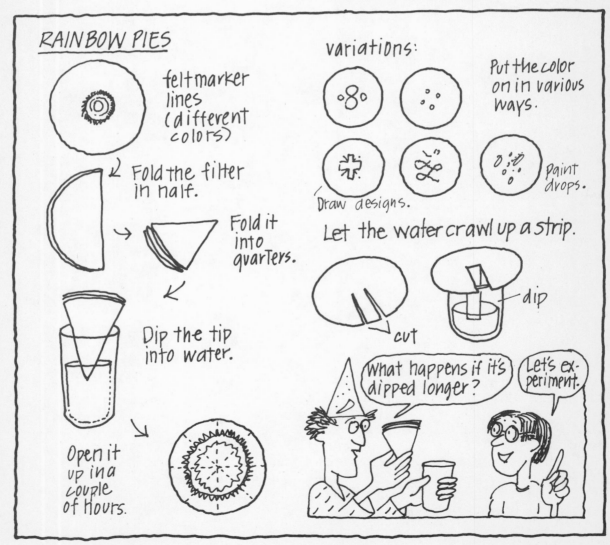

RAINBOW PIES

feltmarker lines (different colors)

Fold the filter in half.

Fold it into quarters.

Dip the tip into water.

Open it up in a couple of hours.

variations:

Put the color on in various ways.

Draw designs.

Paint drops.

Let the water crawl up a strip.

cut

dip

What happens if it's dipped longer?

Let's experiment.

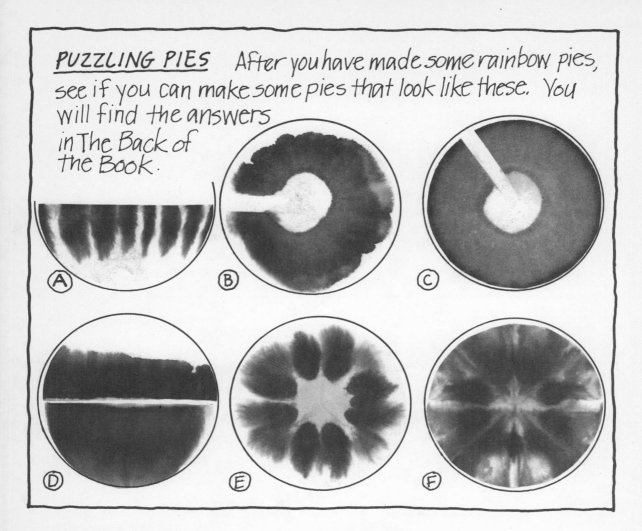

PUZZLING PIES   After you have made some rainbow pies, see if you can make some pies that look like these. You will find the answers in The Back of the Book.

Ⓐ Ⓑ Ⓒ
Ⓓ Ⓔ Ⓕ

Criminal Writing

The FBI uses chromatography as a tool to catch forgers. By testing an ink sample they can identify exactly what kind of pen the ink came from. This test works because every ink breaks apart differently. The bands of exploded color are almost as unique as a fingerprint. This pattern can help identify a pen—a handy thing to know when catching forgers.

Amaze your friends by identifying the criminal pen. Tell some friends that you are an expert in forgery and that you know all there is to know about pens and inks. Tell them you can prove it. Then show them how.

You Will Need
a handful of different black ballpoint pens
paper
filter paper
alcohol or water
a friend

1. Give your friend the pens.
2. Without your knowing, let your friend choose one and have him write on a slip of newsprint paper with the chosen pen.
3. Take the written sample and all the pens. Tell your friend you're going off to the crime lab to run some tests.
4. Test samples of all the inks, each on a different paper strip. Use the

chromatography method explained on page 16. Take care to mark your pens and the samples, so you know which is which.

5. Make a test of the sample written by your friend.

6. Match each of the exploded samples of ink to the original sample of writing. The colors will break up in a characteristic way. This will make it easy to match the ink of the criminal pen with the written sample.

When you have identified the pen, announce that you have the criminal pen in custody. Put your finger on the one that did the writing. Your friend will be amazed.

Criminologists

Criminology is a science that studies crime. It is a combination of biology, chemistry, physics, and bits of other sciences. A criminologist takes a scientific approach to unraveling the evidence in a crime, and tries to reconstruct events. He or she helps police to find out what happened and who is responsible for a crime.

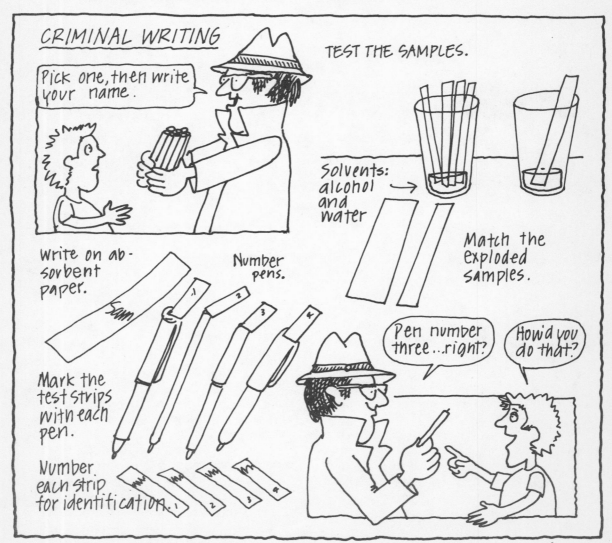

Coming up next:

Fantastic Elastics: building bubbles, observing soap films

Fantastic Elastics

Windows You Don't Have to Wash

Here is a way to make a clear quivering elastic window that does tricks. It will let you blow the biggest bubbles of your life. While you are learning how to use the bubble window, you will learn a lot about soap film and its properties. First make the frame.

You Will Need
some thin cotton string
plastic straw
scissors

1. Cut the straw in half.
2. Cut a string about 20 inches long.
3. Thread it through the two straws.
4. Knot the ends.

If you can't get the soap to stay on the frame, experiment with thicker or thinner string.

Basic Bubble Soap

Now that you have built the window frame, you need to mix up some "window film." Use liquid detergent. The more expensive kinds seem to work best because they are thicker. Here's the formula for basic bubble film.

You Will Need
8 tablespoons liquid detergent
1 quart water
measuring spoons
a quart jar or milk carton
a flat pan (larger than the bubble frame)

MAKE A FRAME

Cut straw.

Knot the string.

Pull the knot inside.

Experiment with windows of different sizes.

BASIC BUBBLE SOAP

1 quart water

Add detergent.

8 tablespoons equals 1/2 cup

Pour in soap.

dish big enough to contain the bubble frame

1. Put the ingredients into the quart container.

2. Stir them with a spoon until they are well mixed.

To make a window you can't wash:

1. Pour the basic bubble soap into a flat-bottom pan. The soap should be at least ½ inch deep.

2. Arrange the frame so you are holding a straw in either hand with the string stretched evenly between them.

3. Dip the frame into the soap. Get the string wet.

4. Pull the frame out slowly so you get a film window stretched along the string. Don't be afraid to let the string go limp. But stretch it taut as you remove it. With a little practice you will have a window you can't wash.

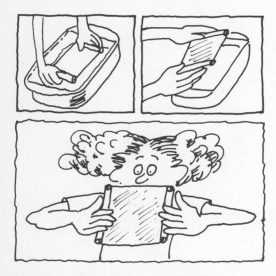

To make the window do tricks:

1. Hold it about waist level.

2. Pull the frame up through the air, while bringing the straws together.

3. When the straws touch, the film will join. The flat film should close to make a big fat bubble, which will float away.

It may take a bit of practice to master making monster bubbles. Stand back when they break, because they explode with a powerful force, and the flying soap might get in your eyes.

MAKE THE WINDOW DO TRICKS

Dip frame.

Pull up, close frame.

Touch straws to release bubble.

Watch out! Big bubbles explode with force.

Here are some more tricks to try with your bubble frame. These experiments will tell you a lot about the properties of soap film.

1. Hold the frame flat. Gently move it up and down, watching the window stretch and return to position. Do you think there are elastic limits for the soap film?

2. Twist the frame. Watch the window stretch and bend. Does the soap film have twisting limits?

3. Put film on the frame. Hold it by only one end. What happens? Why?

4. Make a thread loop. Tie it to the frame so it hangs into the film. Punch out the window in the loop. Why does the loop become a wide open space?

5. Put your hand through the window. It can be done, all the way up to your elbow, if the conditions are right. Experiment to find out what the right conditions are.

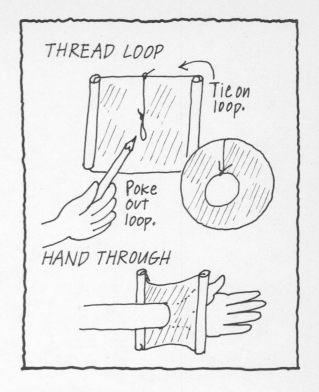

THREAD LOOP

Tie on loop.

Poke out loop.

HAND THROUGH

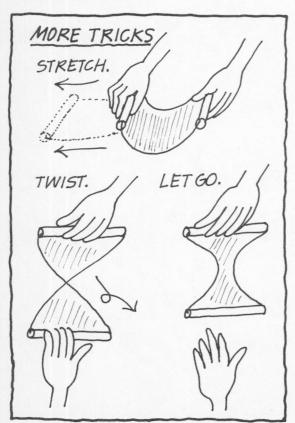

MORE TRICKS

STRETCH.

TWIST.

LET GO.

Soapy Properties

Soap film is sticky. Its molecules are highly attracted to each other. This property causes the film to try to be small. When the film is stretched, the molecules are pulled apart. They can stretch a long way and then pull back to their original position. We call this property elasticity. Rubber bands, underwear, and licorice are also elastic.

wanna see a neat film for a quarter?

Fooling Around with Frames

Give film a frame to cling to and you can be sure it will fit itself to take up the least possible space. It's one material guaranteed free of crumples, rumples, and wrinkles. This shrink-wrap property is fun to play with.

Make any funny-shaped frame and predict the shape that clingy soap film will take on it. Dip it to see if you and the soap film agree on how to form the tightest fit.

You Will Need
some soft, bendable wire
bubble soap
a dish
paper
pencil

1. Make a shape with the wire. Then predict what shape you think the film will take on the frame.

2. Dip the frame in soap so it forms a film over the frame.

3. Lift it out and observe what happened. Was your prediction right? Do you and soap film think along the same lines?

4. Record your predictions and the results for the different frames.

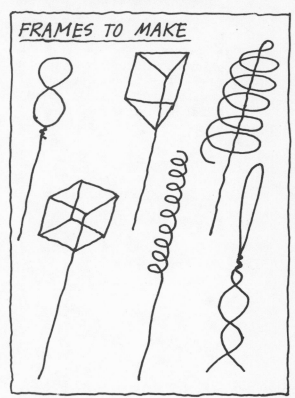

Bubble Colors

When light passes through soap film, it's reflected from both the top and bottom surfaces of the film. Your eye sees a scrambled combination of the two groups of reflected light rays. The light waves don't come out the same way as they go in. This scrambled difference is seen by your eye as colors. The colored band effect is a result of differences in the thickness of the film.

Tabletop Bubbles

Soap film makes wonderful ephemeral sculpture. Of course, it doesn't last a long time (that's what ephemeral means). But it only takes seconds to create a new masterpiece.

You are, no doubt, already an expert at blowing bubbles. But do you know how to blow a half bubble? Or bubbles in single file? Or a bigger-than-your-head bubble? Or a bubble within a bubble within a bubble within a bubble?

These bubbles are not the kind you hang in thin air. These are tabletop creations. You need a smooth, wet surface. Since your bubbles sit quietly, instead of freefalling through the air, these fragile film sculptures have the advantage of living longer.

You Will Need
a bowl or flat tray or a wet, smooth surface
bubble soap
a straw

1. *Half a Bubble:* First wet the surface you will be working on and the outside of the straw. Then dip the straw into the soap. Put it down where you want the bubble and gently blow. Pull out the straw when your dome is as big as you want it to be. Try blowing a bowl-size bubble. Or try one the size of the entire tabletop.

2. *Dome City:* After you have learned how to blow single domes, you are ready to build a whole sparkling cluster of domes that looks like a future city. Try blowing piggyback bubbles.

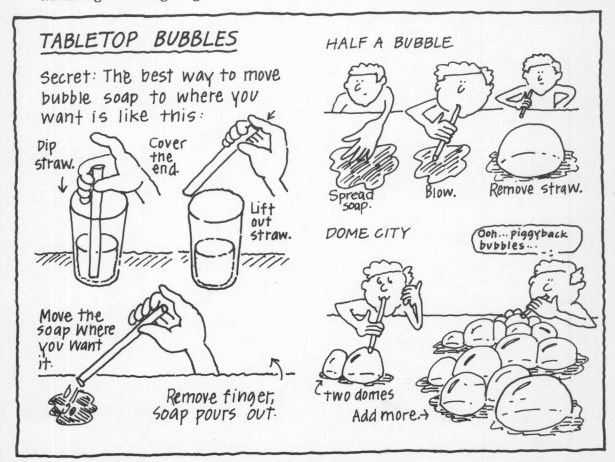

28

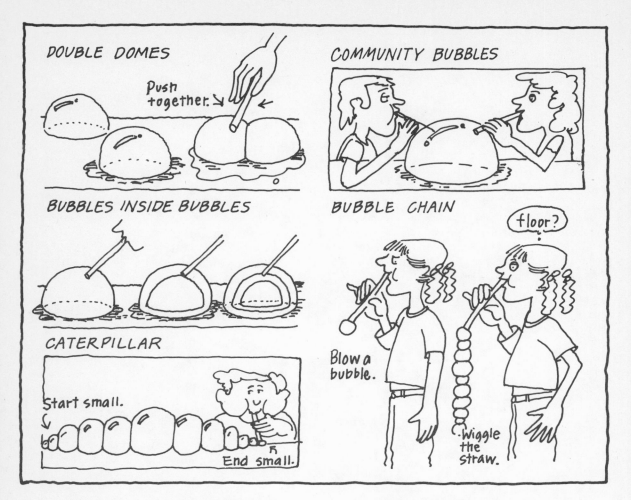

3. *Double Domes:* Blow two bubbles next to each other. Nudge them with your straw so they touch. What shape do they make? What happens at the wall in between? Try three bubbles. Before you blow, predict what shape three will make. Then try it and see.

4. *Bubbles with Inside Bubbles:* Blow a bubble. Stop and start a new one in the center. Be careful not to let the walls touch. You should be able to make three easily before one breaks.

5. *The Caterpillar:* With a bit of bubble-blowing control you should be able to blow a series of bubbles in a row. Start small, get big then small again. This one isn't easy. Why do you suppose bubbles want to form themselves into lumps rather than into lines?

6. *Community Bubbles:* For this bubble extravaganza you need at least one friend with another straw. One person starts the bubble. The other one joins in by putting in all the air he or she can. How big a bubble can you blow? A harder way is for both of you to blow monster bubbles, then see if they can be hooked together.

P.S. Can you think of a way to test whose lungs are larger?

7. *Bubble Chain:* For a long line of stupendous, suspended bubbles, dip your straw and point it toward the floor. Blow a bubble gently. Wiggle the straw to close it. Blow again. Careful, you might wiggle too much and the bubble will get loose. Keep blowing until your chain touches the floor.

Why Bubbles Are Balls

The shape soap film takes is a result of the forces which are at work in and on the film. The reason bubbles are round is because their films are trying to pull themselves into as small a shape as possible. While the film is contracting, the air inside is pushing out in all directions evenly. The forces acting on the film are the same all over it. The shape a material takes when this is the case is always a perfect sphere. Can you explain what makes these bubbles take on these shapes? For the answers see The Back of the Book.

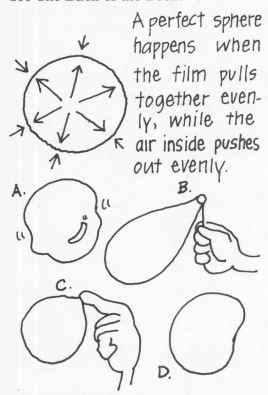

A perfect sphere happens when the film pulls together evenly, while the air inside pushes out evenly.

A.

B.

C.

D.

How Thick Is Thin?

Soap films are thin. Did you know they are about the thinnest thing you can see without a magnifying glass? If you could stack up one soap film on top of another, you would need a pile of 5,000 soap skins just to equal the thickness of an eyelash. Or, thinking of it another way, if you let one hamburger thickness stand for the thickness of a soap film, you would need a pile of 5,000 burgers for them to be visible.

Best Bubble Formula

Dryness is a bubble's number one enemy. Touch a bubble with a dry finger and it breaks. Let it land on a dry surface and it explodes. Bubbles will last much longer on a rainy wet day than on a hot dry day. To test this fact, try blowing bubbles in the shower and in front of a heater.

As water escapes into the air (evaporation), it causes a bubble to pull apart and break. Slow down this drying out process and your bubbles will live longer.

A chemist might do this by adding something to the soap. Glycerin is a chemical used in hand lotions to prevent skin from drying out. Will it work on bubble skin? Experiment with your own soap formula to find out.

You Will Need
a small bottle of glycerin (from the drugstore)
an eyedropper
some small containers (same size) like medicine vials or yogurt pots
bubble soap
a straw
a watch that measures seconds

1. Pour equal amounts of soap into each container.
2. Using the eyedropper, add different amounts of glycerin to each jar. Record what you do, and the results. Later you may want to mix more of the formula that turns out to work best.
3. Test each new formula by blowing a bubble with a straw. Try to blow bubbles of the same size.
4. Time the life of each test bubble. Record the time.

Do great globs of glycerin make the longest-lived bubbles? Experiment to discover the best soap. Use a little more or a little less glycerin until you have the master formula for your super soap. Corn syrup or gelatin powder also work well as antidrying agents. How well, only your experiment can tell.

A Bubble-Blowing Contraption

Here are instructions for a simple bubble-blowing contraption that makes a lot of little bubbles.

You Will Need
a clothespin
a plastic berry basket
scissors

1. Cut the bottom out of the berry basket.

2. Clamp on the clothespin for a handle.

3. Dip the basket in soap film and blow on it, or swish it through the air.

We told you it was simple!

Bubble-Blowing Inventions

Any bubble engineer worth his or her soap knows that there is more than one way to blow a bubble. The first step toward engineering a bubble-blowing invention is to take note of the essential parts of any machine that makes bubbles. There must be a frame on which to hang the soap film, a source of air, and a clear passageway to and from the film so the bubbles can escape free and clear.

Next, a bubble engineer needs some materials to work with. Get all the possible materials you can find, put them together, and look them over. Imagine how each of your materials might work as a part of the bubble-blowing machine. Give your sense of invention some time. (In no time, inventions will bubble forth.)

Put the parts together and test your invention to see if it makes bubbles. Fine tune your bubble invention. A big part of engineering is making changes so that inventions not only work, but work well.

Engineers

Some people wouldn't call engineers scientists at all. But engineers know a lot of science. They are in the business of putting the principles of science to work.

Engineers look like regular people, except they generally have a lump in their clothes where they keep their pocket calculators. (Engineers are very calculating people.) They use calculators to figure out how to do things like building bridges or computers. Or to invent better ways to do things like zippers, cotton candy machines, or bubble-blowing contraptions. Their cars tend to run better than other scientists' cars.

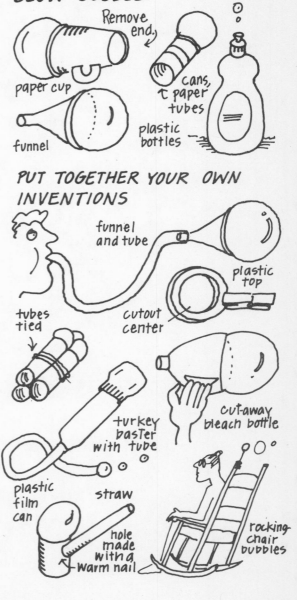

Wet and Creepy

Dippy Designs

You can make wild and wonderful designs and let water do all the work. Well, you do have to do some fancy folding, but here's a simple way to make complex designs in rainbow colors. It relies on the ability of water to crawl through paper with flying colors.

You Will Need
food colors
bowls
newspaper
thirsty paper (white tissue paper or fine-grained paper towels are best)

1. Cover the work space with newspaper. Remember: food color stains. Rubber gloves will keep your hands looking human.
2. Prepare the colors by putting 1/4 cup water and some food color in each bowl. Bright colors make the most brilliant designs.
3. Fold the paper into quarters.
4. Then fold it in half diagonally so that it makes a triangle.
5. Dip each corner in a color.
6. Open it up to see what happened.
7. Set the dippy design in the sun or hang it on a clothesline to dry.

You can get different effects by leaving the paper in the color for a longer time and allowing the color to crawl farther into the paper. Tissue paper gets soft when wet. Don't dye more than half of its surface; otherwise, it is

very hard to open. If it gets too wet, wait until the paper dries before you open it. Double dipping gives interesting color effects too.

DIPPY DESIGN

1/4 cup water plus food color

Unfold a fantastic design.

How you fold the design is important. Here are some easy ways to fold your paper to get interesting designs.

OTHER FOLDS

Dip here↘ or here↘ or roll it into a coil.

Dip here↓ and here.

Fold diagonally, fold again, again. Dip.

Try your own fancy folds.

An Absorbing Challenge

It is easy to make a different design every time you dip. A much harder trick is to duplicate a design without knowing how it was folded. Fold and dip a fancy design, then challenge a friend to make one just the same. It is an absorbing game to play. Here are some dippy challenges to help you get started. There are answers at The Back of the Book.

You'll never guess this fold in a million years.

I think old Wiz is going dippy...

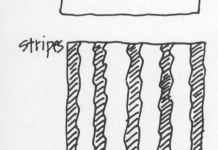

red dot

red cross

bull's-eye

green
yellow

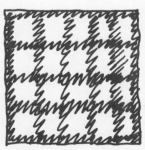

stripes

plaid

dots

35

Great Uphill Water Race

Thrills, chills, and suspense. Who would think a paper towel could be so exciting? This race will test a paper's ability to suck up water and will leave you sitting on the edge of your chair. You will also find out why some paper has such powerful thirst.

You Will Need
paper samples (as many different kinds as you can find — try paper towels, stationery, napkins, tissue, cards)
a glass
water
a pen

1. Cut a race strip from each sample of paper, 1 inch wide by 6 inches long.

2. Give each strip in the race a name or a number to identify it. You might name the strips something descriptive like Glossy, Fuzzy, T.P., or Viva.

3. With a pen, mark a starting line on the glass about 2 inches from the bottom. Mark the finish line about 3 inches above that.

4. Set up the race. Put the strip contestants into the glass. Fold the edges over to balance them.

5. Look over the contestants. Predict the one you think will let water crawl up to the finish line first. Pick your bet for second, third, etc. Write down your predictions.

6. To start the race, pour water into the glass up to the starting line.

7. Wait for the winner to cross the finish line.

8. Note: You may have to give up on some contestants that don't show any signs of ever getting up the gumption to get out of the starting gate. Look your contestants over closely. Do you see any particular property belonging to the fastest, thirstiest towels? (A closer look with a magnifier will help with your observations.)

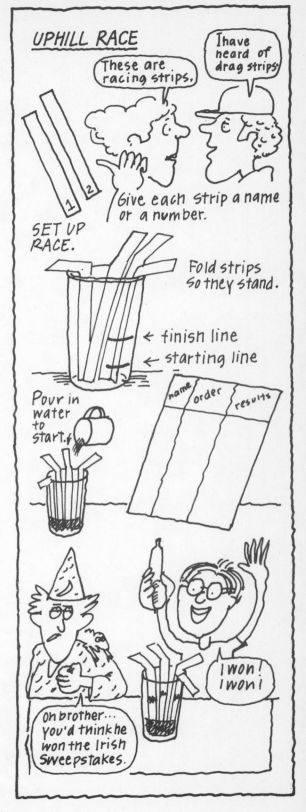

36

Porous

Hold a thin paper up to the light and you will notice that a piece of paper is really a bunch of little fibers all stuck together in a kind of blanket. The kinds of blankets are very different. Some look thick and dense like army blankets. Some look more like a blanket of tangled spaghetti on a plate.

The thirstiest paper is the one with the most holes, or pores, in it. Water is attracted to surfaces. Paper with lots of holes, nooks, and crannies has more surfaces to attract water. So this attraction (known as capillary action) takes place at a faster rate. In short, the more porous, the thirstier.

Water Is Creepy

Remember the time you got a little teeny spot of ink on your best shirt? It started out small, but the next thing you knew it was a big horrible splotch. Then there was the time you spilled a little milk on the tablecloth and pretty soon it was a big puddle. Remember?

The reason for both of these creepy behaviors is the same. It is that water is attracted to all the teeny thread surfaces in fabric. The same attraction that accounts for water's gravity-defying ability to crawl the walls causes water to creep through cloth. And through paper towels. Or anything that contains lots of little spaces.

Micromasterpieces

If you like small stuff, this project is for you. Have you ever tried to write small? Really small? To push your pen and paper to their limits? Experiment with how small a picture you can draw.

You Will Need
a magnifier
pens (fine-tip felt markers)
different kinds of paper

1. Start by drawing some squares measuring a centimeter on a side.
2. Draw something in one of these tiny squares. Use your magnifier to see what happens to the pen line.

3. Keep your art work simple. Half the fun is coming up with big titles for your miniart.

4. Try writing your name. Measure your success by how tall or short you can make your letters and still have them be readable. Less than a millimeter? It might be possible with the right pen and paper.

You will find that the speed of your hand, the rate of ink flow, and the thirstiness of the paper determine a lot about the size of your miniart. After you learn to predict how much the lines expand due to capillary action, you will be able to create some real micromasterpieces.

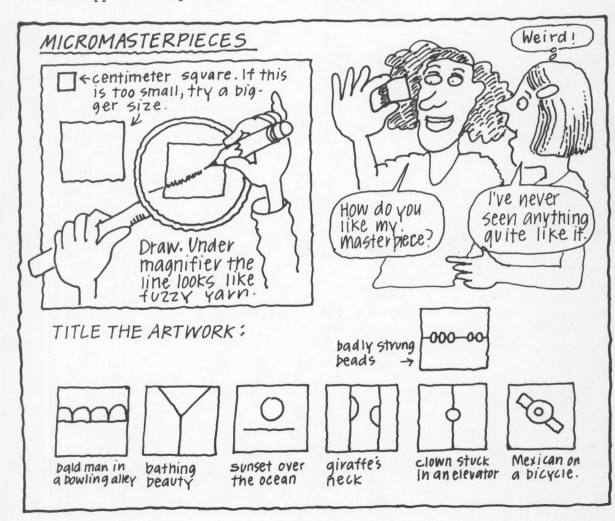

38

Creepy Problem

Not so easy, is it? If you are like most kids, your mind was willing but the pen and ink put up a fight. The creeping action of ink through paper is the enemy. The ink tends to blot out the white spaces and block up the letters, destroying readability.

You have to learn how to outguess capillary action. Draw with lines far enough apart. Leave enough space so your eyes can read what your hand has written.

If capillary action means nothing to you, turn to page 44 for a complete definition.

Small Feat

According to the *Guinness Book of World Records,* Frank C. Watts of Norfolk, England, holds the record for the smallest writing (without any special equipment). In 1968, in front of photographers, he wrote the Lord's Prayer 34 times in a space the size of a postage stamp. It didn't say whether or not he suffered from writer's cramp.

Water Crawls the Walls

Watch water defy gravity and crawl up a wall. Impossible, you say. Not in the least. It's ordinary everyday behavior for water—you just never noticed. If you have never seen water crawl up walls, set up this easy experiment to watch its creepy, crawly, action.

You Will Need
a transparent plastic lid (the kind that comes on coffee cans)
a saucer
food colors
a stapler

1. Cut away the rim from the plastic lid.
2. Cut the lid in half.
3. Put the two sides together so they are flat against each other.
4. Staple (or clip) them so they stay right against each other.
5. Stand this "wall" up in a saucer of water. Beet juice, food color (brightly colored), or washable ink in the water will help you see the crawling action.
6. Step back and watch water crawl the walls.

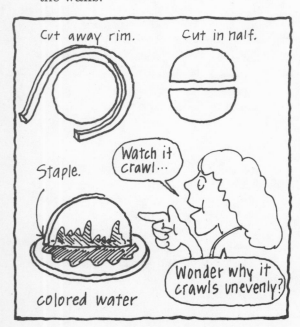

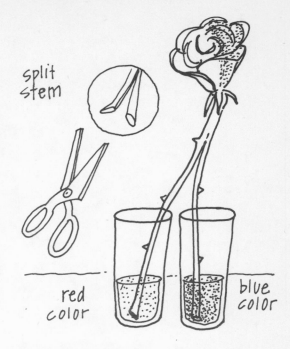

High-Tone Two-Tone Rose

Wouldn't your mom be amazed if you surprised her with a big bicolor bloom for her birthday? When she asks where you got such a rare corsage, tell her it's a blooming miracle. Or you could say, "It was made possible by the results of my scientific research into capillary action." That will surprise her too.

You Will Need
some white flowers (carnations or roses work well)
food color (dark)
a knife
two glasses

1. Set up two glasses of water with different food colors in them.
2. Make a fresh cut at the tip of the stem. Then with a knife or scissors carefully split the stem in half.
3. Put one half into one glass and the other into the second glass. Wait for the two-tone flowers.

Could you make a three-tone tulip? A four-tone daffodil? How about a Fourth of July flower in red, white, and blue?

Sticky Fingerprints

Want to feel atomic forces at work? Pulling apart these print plates will let you feel the sticky power of the atoms in water. Do you feel bonds breaking as you pull the plates apart? You can print with the separated plates to make some interesting designs.

You Will Need
two large clear plastic lids (the kind that comes on coffee cans)
poster paint
white paper

1. Trim the lids so you can put the two surfaces flat against each other.
2. Brush or drop on some poster paint on one side. Start with two colors.
3. Press the other plate against the first. Hold it up to the light and have a wonderful time spreading and mixing the colors by pressing and poking.
4. When you get a design you like, stop. Pull the plates apart. Do you feel the resistance as the atomic bonds are being broken?
5. Press the paper onto the plates. Rub the paper lightly.
6. Pull away the print.

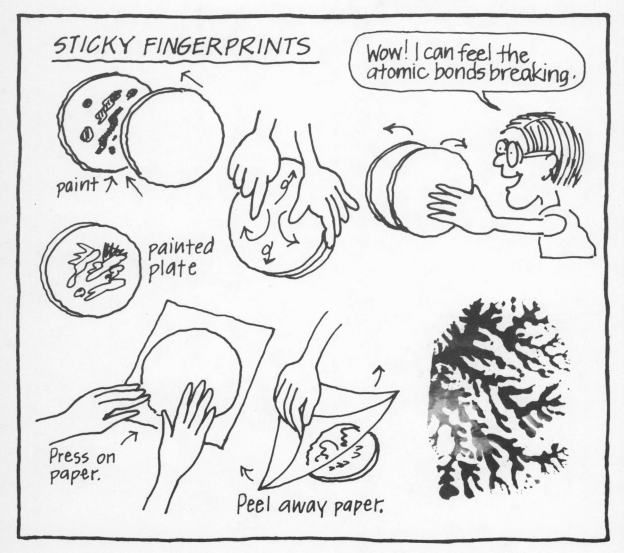

Plant Pipe Patterns

The patterns made by the arrangement of pipes running up and down plants are beautiful. Filling the pipes with colored dye will make the patterns of these tiny plumbing systems more visible. Botanists, the scientists who study plants, call plant pipes the vascular system.

You Will Need
food color
a glass
a celery stalk

1. Fill a glass with a couple of inches of water.
2. Color it with red or blue food color. Make it bright.
3. Slice off the bottom of a stalk of celery.
4. Set it in the dye and wait for the color to travel up the plant's pipes.
5. After the dye is absorbed (a couple of hours) slice off a very thin crosswise section with a very sharp knife. (You might need some adult help to do this.)
6. Hold the section up to the light and look for the pipe pattern.
7. You may want to try cutting the stalk lengthwise to see what that looks like.

The woody strings that get stuck between your teeth when you eat celery are actually plant pipes. It is possible to pull one out and look at it separately.

Try coloring the plumbing systems of other vegetables, like carrots, turnips, or onions. Plants that have their leaves still attached seem to work best.

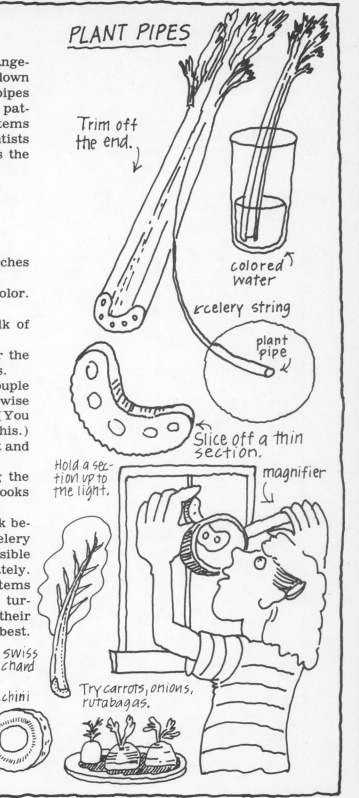

PLANT PIPES

Trim off the end.

colored water

celery string

plant pipe

Slice off a thin section.

Hold a section up to the light.

magnifier

Try carrots, onions, rutabagas.

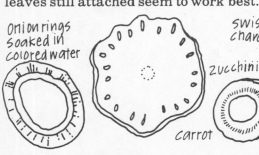

Onion rings soaked in colored water

Swiss chard

Zucchini

Carrot

42

Plant Pipe Puzzle

Plant pipes turn up almost everywhere—on walls, halls, benches, boxes, indoors and out. It is no accident. The grain of wood is the pattern of a tree's pipes. People who work with wood try to let these beautiful patterns show to decorate their work.

Although there are many different plant pipe patterns, an amazing fact is that wood grain is basically the same in every tree. It runs up and down the length of the tree. The differences that show up in grain patterns are the result of the way a log was cut up into boards.

Puzzle over these wood grain designs and see if you can guess how the log was sawed to create these patterns. Answers are in The Back of the Book.

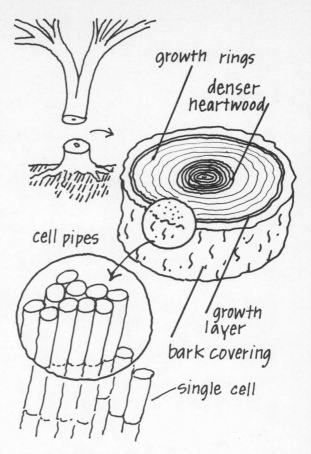

growth rings

denser heartwood

cell pipes

growth layer

bark covering

single cell

A.

B.

C.

D.

Looks like a crosswood puzzle...

How a Tree Grows

Wood is made of a lot of tiny tubes. These hollow, cell-sized pipes are stacked end to end from the roots to the top of the tree. Their job is to carry water and sap around inside the tree. These pipelines are what make the pattern we call wood grain.

The growing part of the tree is just under the bark. It is just one cell thick. Tree rings are caused by yearly differences in growth rates. In the spring a tree grows faster, making light-colored wood. In the summer it grows slower, making darker, denser wood. A count of the rings equals the tree's age.

The heart of a tree is dead. As the tree grows the inner pipes collect more minerals and get squeezed together by the outer layers. The heartwood becomes dense and dark.

Capillary Action

Water crawls up through plant pipes because its adhesive (sticking to other things) force is stronger than its cohesive (sticking to itself) force. Look at a glass of water and you will see that the water lifts itself up a little bit all around the edge. In small tubes where there is a lot of surface for water to grab onto, water can lift itself a very long way. In a very small tube the size of a hair, water can pull itself up to the tops of tall trees.

This property also helps blood surge through tiny hairlike vessels in the body. This crawling ability is called *capillary* (*kap* a larry) *action*. Capillary action will continue to pull water upward against gravity until so much water is pulled up that its weight (downward force) becomes greater than the tugging (upward force) of the capillary action.

Two-Ton Science

Scientists have been known to do strange things. Have you ever heard of one giving a tree a bath? An acid bath? It sounds like some cruel and unusual torture invented by a crazed mind. But, in fact, the man who did this experiment was a lover of trees. A German botanist named Strasburger was fascinated by trees. He was especially curious about a tree's talent for lifting massive amounts of water. Trees perform this weight-lifting feat with no pump to push the tree juices skyward. Some people thought it was magical. Strasburger thought not.

He suspected that the secret was in the tree's huge system of tiny pipes. And he figured, if this were true, then fluids ought to circulate through a dead tree just as easily as they do through a living one.

Strasburger decided to perform an experiment to test his theory. He cut down a two-ton tree. He then set it in a giant bath of picric acid, powerful stuff that will kill just about anything. Within a week the tree was dead. But the acid was still moving from the bucket at the base to the leaves at the top. He proved that the tree's circulation system carried on whether the tree was dead or alive. His theory that the secret of moving tree blood is in the pipes was correct.

Today we know that it is water's ability to climb up the walls of tiny tubes (capillary action) that accounts for the circulation of tree blood. We can thank Strasburger for his acid test.

Botanists

Botanists are people who study plants. They collect, classify, and study all sorts of plants: mushrooms, pond slime, and giant sequoias, to mention a few. Botanists have learned how to grow square tomatoes, cabbage roses, and Golden Delicious apples. Botanists often have dirt underneath their fingernails and tend to wear no-nonsense shoes.

44

Coming up next:

Water's Weird Skin: testing surface tension

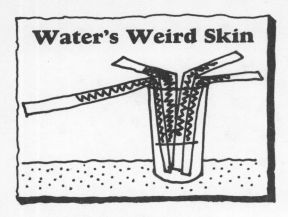

Water's Weird Skin

A Tall Drop of Water

All drops are not created equal. An equal amount of water takes on various shapes depending on what it has its feet on. Do some drippy observation to find out how to create a tall drop of water.

You Will Need
an eyedropper
paper samples
water

1. Cut some small samples of paper.
2. Put a drop of water on each sample. Try to squeeze out the same size drops.
3. Compare the shapes the drops make.
4. Put them in order, from flat to tall.

Squeeze out drops of equal size.↘

Cut paper.↗

Science for drips.

What paper base gives you the tallest drop? Can you come up with a theory that accounts for drops with different shapes?

Try samples of: paper towel, writing paper, Kleenex, newsprint, onion skin, wax paper. Test papers that are fuzzy, slick, thin, fat. Use as many different kinds of paper as you can find.

It's a battle of forces.

Cohesion vs. adhesion.

Cohesion, Adhesion

Water is constantly and continuously trying to pull itself together. This is why it bulges up into a drop. This sticking together force is called *cohesion*. When water touches a surface, it is attracted to that surface. This sticking-to-other-things force is *adhesion*. Water is attracted to different surfaces by differing amounts. Really attractive surfaces make water spread way out.

In the case of a drop on paper, adhesion causes the drop to flatten out. The more attractive the paper surface, the flatter the drop.

Rarely Round

Spheres appear in the form of gas bubbles in soda pop, bubbles in ocean froth, or planets in space.

Perfect spheres are rare in the natural world. More often you will see almost spherical or somewhat round shapes in nature—drips, drops, or blobs. Drips are spheres forced out of a round shape by gravity. Drops are spheres pulled out of shape as they drag along a surface.

46

A Brush of Fresh Air

Put a drop of water on a piece of paper and watch what happens. You will notice that water doesn't take that sort of treatment lying down. It gathers itself up into a bump.

Here is a way to make some interesting designs and push water around, and you'll discover how much force it takes to make water flat.

You Will Need
some paper
food color or washable ink
water
a straw
newspaper

1. Before you start, cover the work surface with newspaper. Food color stains. Be careful.

2. Mix the color from the bottle with water in equal amounts.

3. Dip the straw into the colored water. Put your finger over the top end.

4. Put some drops of color on the paper. Bumpy, aren't they?

5. Now apply some force in the form of blowing these colors across the page. You'll find you have to apply a strong stream of air through the straw to break up those sticky bumps.

6. Observe what happens when you turn off the air. Can you ever completely flatten the liquid? What happens to the liquid when the air stream stops? Why?

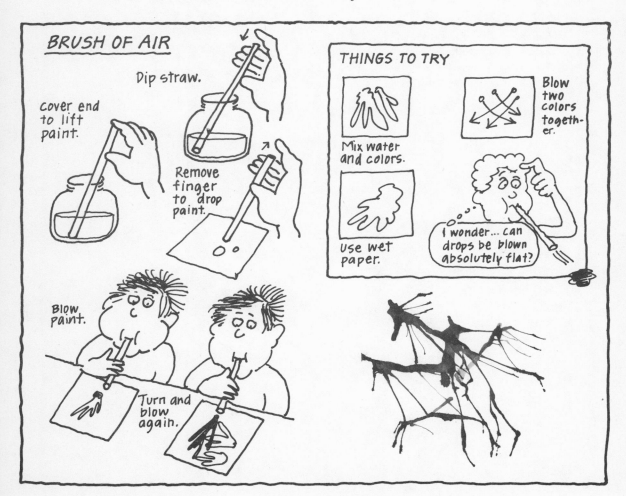

Drop Racing

Wax paper is something most people can't get excited about. That's because they don't know it can be the base for a fascinating game of speed and skill. The name of the game is drop racing. It's a fascinating activity for the fluid scientist. The game takes advantage of wax paper's special waterproof property, making it a perfect material for forming big bulging racing drops. And its easy-to-scratch surface is excellent for setting up a race track.

You Will Need
wax paper
water
a spoon
a paper punch
a watch

1. Cut a sheet of wax paper about 12 inches by 14 inches.

2. With the handle end of the spoon, draw out some maze lines (see illustration).

3. Punch some hole traps for the water drops.

4. Spoon a water drop onto the starting place.

5. Pick up the maze and send the drop rolling along the maze way. Move it along until it reaches the center.

Challenge a friend to a water drop race. Keep track of the time to determine the winner.

Nonabsorbent means waterproof.

DROP RACING

Draw the maze. 14" 12"

A blunt pencil or pen will also draw lines.

finish

Punch hole traps.

Put a drop at the starting gate.

Hey! Your time is up!

Wow! Better than Space Invaders.

Roll the drop to finish.

Wiggle paper.

Fuller Than Full

Bet you have never filled a glass full of water.

Absolutely full?

Unless it's filled over the top, a glass is not as full as it can be. With some careful pouring you can pile up more water in a glass than you ever thought possible.

You Will Need
a tall narrow glass
paper towels
an eyedropper
water
food color

1. Set the glass on a paper towel. Fill it with water, without spilling any.

2. Add a few drops of food color so you can really see the water.

3. Are you sure it's full? If the water level isn't up to the rim, pour in a bit more to bring it up to the top.

4. Do you think it's full now? Yes? Well, get ready to be amazed. Get an eyedropper.

5. Do you care to predict how many drops it will hold?

6. Write down your prediction. Then keep adding drops until you know it's full. (Full is when the water spills over the rim and trickles onto the towel.)

Meniscus

Whether you know it or not, you have made a *meniscus* (meh *niss* cuss). Put your eye to rim level to get a better look at it. Meniscus is a scientific word to describe the bulge of water piled up above the rim of the glass. This strange hump is held in place by water's tendency to stick to itself, or, what scientists call its surface tension. The word meniscus also refers to the shape that water takes when it fills a container not so full. In this case, the water surface curves the opposite way.

Surface Tension

Go ahead and test the water bulge at the top of the glass with a poke of your finger. It gives like jello. It is as if there is a skin holding the water in place. There is.

An invisible skin is formed at the boundary of the liquid by the stickiness of the water molecules and their attraction to each other. Scientists call these attachments "bonds." They are tight, elastic, and hard to break. This property of water is called surface tension. It allows water to pile up over the top of the glass forming a bulge. Until the pressure gets to be too much. Then the skin gives way, and the water surface breaks and it spills over the side.

In a liquid state, water can form bonds with four neighbor molecules.

surface

At the surface, there are no neighbor molecules above, so water bonds to the sides and below. These strong bonds pull water into a tight, taut skin.

Brawny Bonds

The tight, elastic bonds that hold water molecules together are so strong that you can float a piece of metal on their surface with a bit of practice.

Then with a common everyday chemical you can loosen the bonds and watch the metal sink.

You Will Need
a bowl of water
a paper clip
an eyedropper
liquid detergent or soap

1. Bend the paper clip so that one end forms a handle.
2. Carefully set the clip so it sits flat on the surface of the water.
3. Remove your fingers and watch it sit on the water's skin.
4. Carefully let a few drops of soap or detergent slide down the side of the dish. Watch closely. Amazing isn't it?

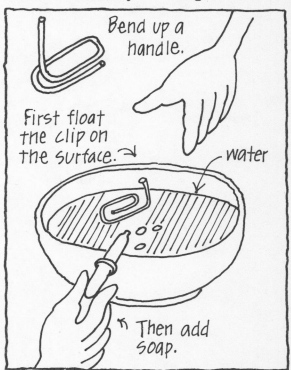

Bend up a handle.

First float the clip on the surface.

water

Then add soap.

Rearranging Molecules

The molecules of soap are highly attracted to the molecules of water. When soap molecules touch water they want to stick to water. Or more scientifically speaking, they form a molecular attachment called a bond. The molecular arrangement of the water is actually changed right before your very eyes.

The tight, elastic water-to-water bonds are changed to a looser soap and water arrangement. The surface tension loosens. The new bonds are not strong enough to hold up the metal. The clip sinks.

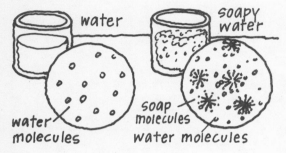

Surface Swifties

Detergents are made up of molecules that show special behavior toward water molecules. A part of each detergent molecule likes very much to stick to water molecules. We say it's hydrophilic. But the other part of the detergent molecule can't stand water molecules and always tries to stay out of contact with them. It's hydrophobic.

When a drop of detergent is placed on the surface of water, all its molecules quickly try to arrange themselves so that their water-loving parts touch the water but their water-hating parts do not.

The best way for detergent molecules to do this is for the drop to spread out across the surface of the water. The detergent molecules line up in formation on the surface, with their hydrophilic parts in contact with the water, and their hydrophobic parts sticking upwards. It's sort of like roosters with their tails up. Scientists call this formation a monolayer.

Streaming Colors

It looks like a dish full of regular milk, until it bursts into streams of exploding colors that mix and twist in a most amazing way. This show is put on by liquid detergent's fast action as it passes through fluids.

You Will Need
a bowl
milk
food color
liquid detergent

1. Pour about an inch of milk into a bowl.
2. Wait until the milk is still. Gently drop some dots of food color into the milk.
3. Quietly pour a stream of detergent down the side of the bowl.
4. Watch the colors explode.

How long does the swirling continue? Do you have any idea why it stops? Try pouring in two streams of detergent.

Atomic Agitation

Want to see molecules in motion? Actually a molecule is way too small to see, but you can easily see evidence of molecular motion. All it takes is some blobs of dye, water molecules in a glass, and some time.

You Will Need
a clear glass
water
food color or ink

1. Fill the glass with water.
2. Add some drops of food color to the water. Use two different colors.
3. Watch what happens while things settle down.
4. Leave the glass in a quiet place. Come back and check it in a couple of hours.

drops of food color →

water

CHECK AGAIN LATER.

Diffusion

Molecules are constantly in motion. As they move they bump into each other and push each other around, rather like billiard balls or bumper cars. After a little while all this atomic pushing and shoving mixes the molecules up until they have made a uni-form mixture (all the same). The scientific word for this atomic self-stirring is *diffusion* (dif *few* shun). Diffusion explains how dye can mix itself in a glass. It also accounts for a lady's perfume spreading across a room.

Molecular Motion

The molecules that make up the water in the old swimming hole, in mysterious fog, and in thin ice are all the same water molecule, H_2O, the old rabbit ear molecule.

The difference between water, mist, and ice is movement. Molecules are always moving. The difference is how thickly they cluster and how fast they move.

A scientist describes these differences in speed as three different states of matter. These three states are solid, liquid, and gas. Imagine, if you can, that matter is like a soccer game. Every person represents a molecule. The players on the field are spread out and moving fast. They are gas. The folks in the seats are packed closely and are vibrating a bit, but not much. They are solid.

The people streaming through the aisles to the hot dog stands are in between. They are moving faster than solid but not as fast as gas. They are packed together less than the solid but closer than the gas. They are liquid.

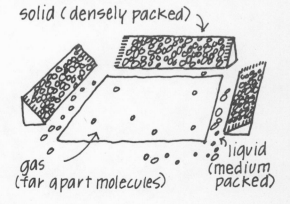

solid (densely packed) ↓

gas (far apart molecules)

liquid (medium packed)

Coming up next:
The Unmixables:
investigating immiscible liquids

The Unmixables

Puddle Paper

Rainbows that form in puddles have wonderful colors and intricate swirly patterns. Like all rainbows, they are wild and elusive things and not very portable. But there is a way to capture a colorful oily film on paper. The results are swirly rainbow patterns you can hang on your wall or wrap a package with. No two designs turn out the same. Plus it's a fun way to study the properties of fluids that just won't mix.

You Will Need
paper (white typewriter paper is fine)
an old flat pan (bigger than the paper)
paint thinner or turpentine
oil-base paint (you can use model paint
   or any leftover samples you find
   around the house)
a pencil
salad oil
newspapers
containers (to mix paint)
a funnel
paper towels
an apron

1. This is a messy project, so cover your work space well with newspapers.
2. Thin the paint so it is a watery consistency. Try mixing one part paint with one part thinner to start off with. Thin at least two colors.
3. Rub the pan with a thin coat of oil to make cleanup easier. Pour about an inch of water into the pan.
4. Pour a little paint into the pan. When it floats to the top, swirl it around with a pencil. It should be thin enough to make a floating film on the water.
5. Add dots of another color. Gently swirl it around until you get a design you like.
6. Lay a sheet of paper down flat on the surface of the liquid.
7. Pick up a corner of the paper. Carefully pull up the whole sheet. The oily swirls will stick to the paper immediately. Don't let it get soaked and soggy.
8. Let it drip for a moment and lay it aside to dry. Drying will take from 30 minutes up to a day, depending on the weather (humidity) and how thick the paint is.

Try another one. When the water gets muddy-looking, pour it out and replace it with fresh water. Pour the mixture into an empty container with a lid. Put it in the garbage can. **Do not pour** this mixture down a drain. Change the designs by adding more colors. Or, mix thick and thin colors. Try dropping in some dots of thinner to separate colors.

Insoluble Problem

Imagine that you are flying exploratory missions for a starship on a distant planet. The engines on the scout vehicle have developed problems and you have crash-landed on a planet's desert surface. Drat, the sharp crystal grit in the atmosphere has fused the power plant. It looks like you're down for good. What's more, the communication system has been destroyed in the crash. There is no hope that you can get to high ground where you can use the portable communicator to send out a beam for help. And you know if you sit back and wait for help you face certain death.

PUDDLE PAPER

Thin paint. More colors make more interesting effects.

Oil the pan. Pour in water. ↓

Gently pour paint in pan.

newspaper for easy cleanup

Swirl the paint.

Add more colors.

Lay paper flat.

Pull up paper.

Let paper drip.

Let it dry.

VARIATIONS

dot of color

Add dots in dots to form rings.

thick color   with very thin color

Blow holes in paint.

drops of thinner

for open spaces ↗

Dip sections of paper ↓

Try metallic paint from model shops.

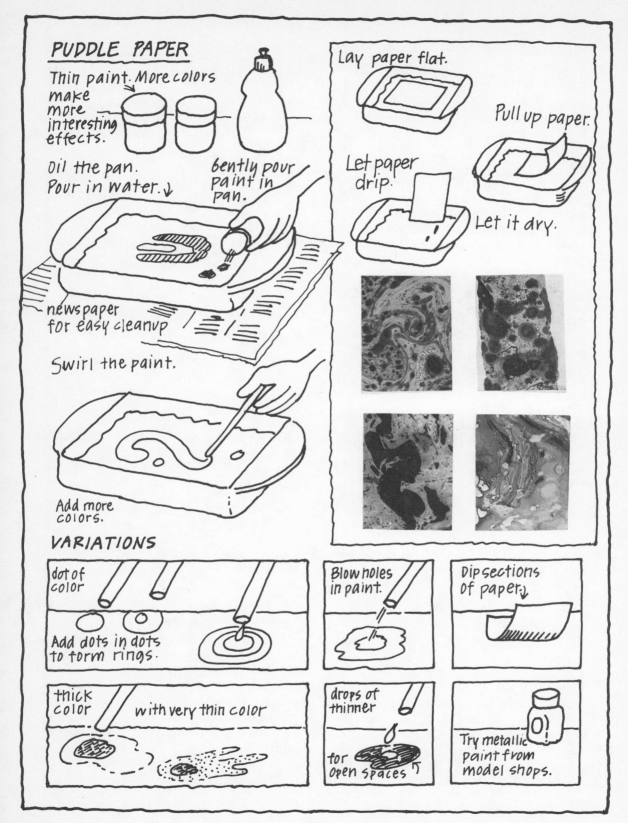

You check your survival gear and decide to go for help. There are two things you must have. One is water. You figure you have enough for six hours on the ferocious floor of the dry planet. The other is oil—the special oil that keeps the acid air from burning through your space suit and eating into your skin. Without the suit's protection you are a goner in a few minutes.

You reach for the precious liquids and to your horror find out one of the two containers has sprung a leak and is draining away. Reacting instantly, you pour the precious water into the oil jar. As you're putting the cork on, you remember the antiacid substance is poison when swallowed. And water will ruin the skin of your space suit.

What are you going to do? Can you get the oil out separately? Or the water? All is not lost. There is a way. Can you think what it might be? Find the answer at The Back of the Book.

Fat Trap

Can you invent a device that will let you pour pure gravy and leave the grease behind? Do you have any good ideas how this miracle might be accomplished? Turn to The Back of the Book for one possible solution.

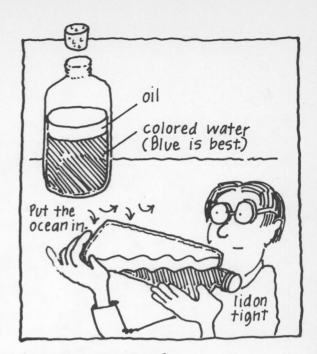

Breakers in a Bottle

If you ever wished you had something that didn't fall apart, this project is for you. It is impossible to get these two liquids to separate and mix into each other. No matter how hard you try. Observing the nature of these unmixable fluids is fascinating. In fact, you can find this very same toy in stores, for sale to adults.

You Will Need
a bottle (the flatter the better) with a tight-fitting lid
water
food color
cooking oil

1. Fill the bottle half full of water.
2. Add a few drops of food color. Make it a deep rich color you like.
3. Pour on a layer of oil.
4. Put the cap on tight.
5. Tip the bottle to put this ocean in motion, and see what happens.

When you get tired of your ocean, change it by adding a few drops of liquid detergent. The detergent will cause the two liquids to mix together, forming an emulsion.

Immiscible

Oil and water never mix. The scientific word for this separate state of affairs is that they are *immiscible* (eh *miss* able). You know this if you have ever tried to make oil and vinegar salad dressing stick together. The two liquids just won't mix. Oil will always float stubbornly to the top and sit there. It always sits on top because it is the lighter liquid.

By giving it a hard shake, you can get the oil to break into the water. Look closely and you'll notice that it's just broken into little bits, or droplets. It hasn't actually mixed. The droplets are suspended in the water. Give them time and they will run together again. *Coalesce* (ko ah *less*) is the scientific word for this running together.

Bead in a Bottle

This is one kind of marble you don't have. It's a marble made of 100 percent cooking oil. It's not much good to play with, but it is very interesting to observe. It looks like a mysterious planet suspended in space. And it will explain more about the forces that shape all the things that float.

You Will Need
rubbing alcohol
cooking oil
food color
water
an eyedropper
a half-pint bottle (the very best kind of bottle to use is a half-pint flask)

1. Fill the bottle about half full of water.

2. Add some blue or green food color.

3. Pour in a few spoonfuls of oil.

4. Add some alcohol. Notice what happens to the shape of the oil.

5. Keep adding alcohol until the oily layer becomes a perfect sphere.

BEAD IN A BOTTLE

Flat bottles work best. →

oil

water + blue or green color

Add alcohol.

Watch the oil change shape.

Looks more like a mushy marble.

Look! Bead in a bottle.

57

Bead in a Bottle:
The Principle of the Thing

The shape of things is determined by the forces acting on them. You can change the shape of the oil from a flat layer to a sphere by controlling the forces pushing on it. When the oil floats to the top, air pushes on it from above. And the alcohol pushes on it from below. It naturally takes the shape of a layer. When you add alcohol, the water mixture becomes lighter (less dense). So the oil begins to sink into the alcohol and water mixture, because it has gotten heavier in comparison. As the oil sinks, it changes shape. The alcohol/water liquid is now pushing on it equally from all directions. This causes the oily layer to take the shape of a ball.

Oil knows which way is up.

On Top of Things

You can prove this title by turning the Breakers in a Bottle upside down. Oil goes right to the top.

1. Give the bottle one good shake. What happens to the oil and water? How many seconds does it take to return to normal?

2. Now give it three good shakes. Do you see any difference in the size of the oil droplets? How many seconds does it take to return to normal?

3. Get carried away and give it ten good shakes. (You do have the lid on tight, don't you?) What size are the droplets now? How many seconds does it take to return to normal this time? How small can you smash up the oil? Do you think there is a limit to the smallness of the oily bits? Do you think you can shake it hard enough to break up the oil into the water forever?

ONE SHAKE

Time the return to normal.

TWO SHAKES

TEN SHAKES

Look closely. Is there any order to the bubbles?

All Wet Sandwich

Have you ever heard of a wet sandwich? It's not on most restaurant menus. However, this liquid demonstration does look good enough to eat. And it lets you observe the properties of immiscible liquids.

You Will Need
a tall slender bottle (the taller and thinner, the better)
cooking oil
rubbing alcohol
food colors

1. Fill the bottle about 1/3 full of water. Color it with some drops of food color.

2. Slowly add a layer of oil. It is best if you pour it down the side of the bottle.

3. Gently fill it to the top with the alcohol. Add a few drops more of a different food color.

4. Put the lid on the liquid sandwich.

With some careful handling, you can make the water and the alcohol trade places. Carefully turn the bottle on its side. Be careful when you tip the liquid. If you let the oil layer barrier down, the two layers will disappear into each other. They are what's called miscible fluids.

Floating Problem

Two liquids that will mix are *miscible* (*miss* a bl). Alcohol and water are two miscible liquids; when you put them together they do mix. Believe it or not, they mix better if you pour one in the jar first. Can you guess which one? What might account for this strange behavior? See The Back of the Book for the answer.

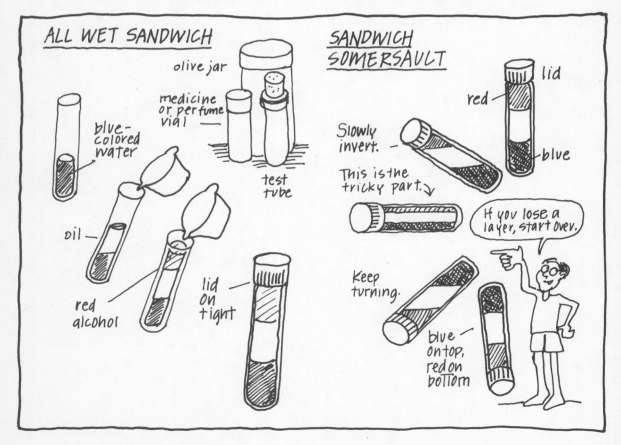

ALL WET SANDWICH

olive jar

medicine or perfume vial

blue-colored water

test tube

oil

red alcohol

lid on tight

SANDWICH SOMERSAULT

lid

red

blue

Slowly invert.

This is the tricky part.

If you lose a layer, start over.

Keep turning.

blue on top, red on bottom

Picture-Lifting Liquid

Solvents have the power to break substances apart, right before your very eyes. Here is a formula for a solvent solution that breaks apart printer's ink. The loosened ink can be rubbed right off the page onto another sheet of paper. You can actually lift pictures right out of a newspaper to print your own cartoons, cards, or stationery.

You Will Need
turpentine
a glass jar with a tight-fitting lid
a bit of hand soap
water
newspapers
scissors
a paint brush
a spoon

1. Pour 1/2 cup of water into a jar.
2. Add 2 tablespoons of turpentine.
3. Add a bit of soap about the size of a pencil eraser.
4. Put the lid on and shake it well, so that the two liquids mix.
5. Find a picture from a newspaper or magazine you want to lift. Cut it out.
6. Brush the front of the picture with the lifting liquid.
7. Put the cutout face down on a clean sheet of white paper. Cover it with another sheet.
8. Rub the cutout with the back of a spoon. Rub hard to make a good transfer.
9. Peel back the cutout and the covering paper. You should have a good impression of the original.

The printer's ink gets harder to dissolve as it ages. Use recent newspapers for the darkest and best results. Colored comics can also be lifted.

A Sticky Spot

Yuck! Somehow you sat in a big wad of bubble gum. You haven't any idea how it got there. Of course, you have on your best pants. If you have tried rubbing and scrubbing bubble gum with soap and water, you know that doesn't work. You've got a really sticky problem and you need a solution.

You need a solvent solution. Rub the gummy spot with a dab of spot remover, and the gum will come away from the cloth almost effortlessly. A solvent is a liquid that has the power to dissolve another substance.

You need to know that not all solvents work on all substances. Water is so attractive that it comes close to dissolving most substances. That's why it is sometimes called the universal solvent. But water won't work on bubble gum. So try some other chemicals that have solvent properties. Carbon tetrachloride is the solvent which is usually sold in stores as "spot remover." Gasoline, turpentine, and acetone are also solvents.

Solvent Action

Substances are made up of tiny particles called molecules. These molecules are held together by attractive forces called bonds. Think of bonds as a kind of molecular glue. These attractive bonds can be very sticky as in the case of bubble gum. Or very, very sticky as in the case of an iron bar. Or not so sticky, as in the case of a piece of chalk. Besides holding materials together, these bonds can attract substances to other substances, such as bubble gum to your pants.

A solvent (usually a liquid) has the power to take apart (dissolve) molecular bonds. The molecules of bubble gum are attracted to the molecules of your pants. When you introduce some solvent, the situation changes. Suddenly the bubble gum is more attracted to the molecules of the solvent than to the molecules of your pants. The bubble gum molecules let go of your pants and link up with the solvent. Your troubles are over, at least as far as your pants are concerned.

61

Coming up next:

Movies on the Brain: looking into your persistent vision

Movies on the Brain

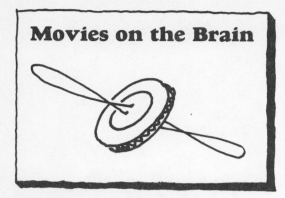

Brand Your Eyeballs

Did you know you can see things with your eyes closed? You don't have to be dreaming either. Try it. As the old saying goes, "Seeing is believing." Here is an experiment to prove it.

You Will Need
white paper
felt markers, black, plus some colors
a bright light

1. Draw a black cross in the middle of a sheet of paper.
2. Put it under a bright light.
3. Stare at it for 30 seconds. Don't blink. Keep your eyes steady.
4. When the count is up, close your eyes. Look toward the light. What do you see?

Try the experiment several ways. Give your eyes a few minutes to rest. Draw a colored cross. Or draw a different-shaped figure with a couple of colors. What do you see with a red cross? A blue one? A green one? Try testing a friend with the same figures. Does everyone see the same colors?

Persistent Vision

Your eyes see by means of a coating of light-sensitive cells. This coating is called the *retina* (*ret* in ah). When light hits the cells they get excited, and a message of this excitement is sent to the brain. It takes a bit of time to do

this and for the cells to calm down again, so the light picture that they get doesn't vanish instantly. It lasts for a fraction of a second. This holding action is called *persistent vision.*

Seeing spots is sometimes an example of persistent vision. It is especially true with really bright lights. Can you remember the last time you were zapped with a flash from a camera? You saw spots for a long time after the flash went off. Glance at a sunset and afterward you will see an orange ball, or a couple of them when you close your eyes. Perhaps you have noticed something funny happen after you stare out the window. When you look away, the window shape is still there. These are all examples of your persistent vision.

This works best in a dark room.

Wow! I can "see" with my eyes shut.

Pressing Patterns

The light-sensitive cells that coat the back of your eye are also sensitive to pressure. You may have discovered that if you gently press your eyelids you will see colored dots and patterns. (A dark place is the best place to try this.) You are actually stimulating the color-sensitive cells in the back of your eyeballs. Your brain reads the pressing messages as colors and patterns.

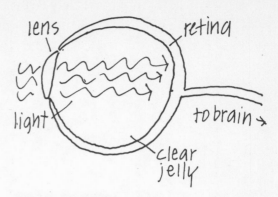

lens • retina • light • to brain → • clear jelly

Inside the Eye

If you could take out one of your eyes, it would look a lot like a ping-pong ball, except one end would be sliced off and replaced with a clear window. The window is called the lens. Attached to the other end is a white cord that plugs the eye into the brain. This cord is called the optic nerve.

Inside the ball is clear, colorless jellylike stuff that lets light through and keeps the eye puffed up to the right shape. Just behind the lens is a set of curtains that open up and close down the amount of light getting in. You need this so you don't scorch the back of your eyeballs with too much light. This is the colored part, called the iris.

In the middle of the iris is the black part of the eye. It is actually just a hole. Light passes through this hole on its way to the back of the eyeball. The back of your eye (the retina) is coated with a light-sensitive material. Its job is to change the patterns of light to electrical impulses. These impulses are sent to your brain along the optic nerve. The brain decodes and makes sense out of the impulses.

The retina doesn't take a constant picture. It takes a lot of separate pictures. In fact, it sends about 12 pictures a second to your brain. Your brain blends the separate pictures together into what seems like a constant picture.

Minimovies

Did you ever want to put some action into your drawings? This is an easy and fast way to make your own animations. It is so much fun that if you are like most kids, you will want to draw up a whole pile of these little movies before you put your pencil down.

You Will Need
some plain white paper (thin enough to see through for tracing)
a pencil

1. If you are using typewriter paper, fold it into four equal sections crosswise. You will end up with some strips that measure about 2½ inches wide by 8½ inches long.
2. Fold a strip in half crosswise.
3. On the bottom half make a drawing. A person's face is a good subject.
4. Bring the back half over so that it covers your drawing.
5. Trace the person as exactly as you can, except you will need to change a little something about it. (Make one eye wink, or change the mouth from a smile to a frown. Or perhaps a big fat fly lands on his nose, causing him to look cross-eyed. Or maybe the full moon is out and he becomes a beast.) You decide. It's your movie.
6. To animate the person, flip over the back flap. Put your pencil along the bottom edge and roll the top picture so that it curls around the pencil. Roll it tightly, all the way up to the fold.
7. Hold the back flap down with one hand. Curl and uncurl the top flap to show the bottom picture. Do this as fast as you can. With fast curling and uncurling action, you'll get an animated face that winks, blinks, and grows bald.

Try another. There are all sorts of little movies you might make. Here are some possible titles: Innocent-Minded Harvey, Horror in the Night, The Winking Cone Head, Running Dog, Mt. St. Helens, The Explosion, The Car Crash of the Century. Your only limit is your imagination and your drawing ability. You might even consider making minimovies in color.

MINIMOVIES

8½ X 11 paper   Cut a strip.   Fold over, trace, but change one feature.   Tracing is easiest in a window.   To animate, curl and uncurl the top flap.

Draw a person.

MINI MOVIES (SPECIAL EFFECTS)

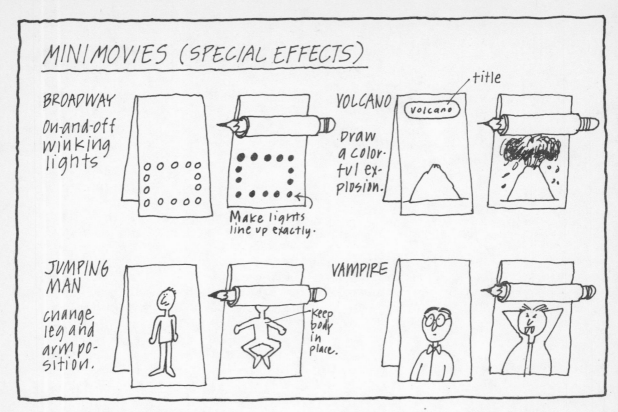

BROADWAY
On-and-off winking lights

Make lights line up exactly.

VOLCANO
Draw a colorful explosion.

title
volcano

JUMPING MAN
change leg and arm position.

Keep body in place.

VAMPIRE

Fool-Your-Eyes Flipper

If you show your eyes two different pictures really fast you can fool yourself into thinking you are seeing both pictures at once. This contraption has an old time name; it's called a thaumatrope. It is one of the early inventions that led to movies.

You Will Need
stiff paper
a pencil with an eraser
a pushpin
a pencil or pen

1. Cut out a 2-inch square of paper.
2. Draw a fish on one side and a bowl on the other.
3. Stick the square to the side of the eraser with a push pin.
4. Hold the pencil up between your hands. Roll it back and forth so both sides of the paper flip into view. When you flip fast enough, the fish will appear to get wet.

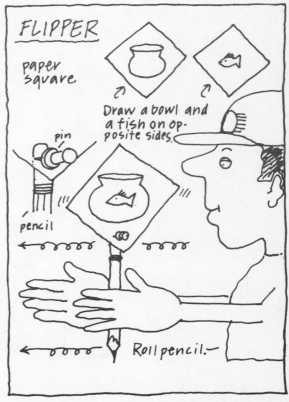

FLIPPER
paper square

Draw a bowl and a fish on opposite sides.

pin

pencil

Roll pencil.

Color Changer

Mix colors right in your eye. That's right! And you don't need any messy brushes, paint, or pots of water. Perform this optical trick by making a spinning toy that hums and buzzes and is lots of fun all by itself. When you color it, the spinning action will cause two colors to make a third right before your very eyes and switch back in a flash.

You Will Need
colored markers or crayons
thin cardboard
scissors
glue
string
a nail
a pencil compass

1. Cut a cardboard circle measuring 3½ inches across. Trace the circle pattern in the illustration onto a piece of white paper.

2. Color it. While you are doing this, predict what colors you will see when you spin it.

3. Glue it onto the cardboard. Smooth out the wrinkles. Rubber cement is the best glue for this job.

4. Carefully punch the holes with a sharp pencil or a nail. Make sure that they are centered. Otherwise, you will have some trouble spinning your color changer.

5. Cut a yard length of heavy soft string or strong yarn.

6. Push the string through the holes. Knot the ends together.

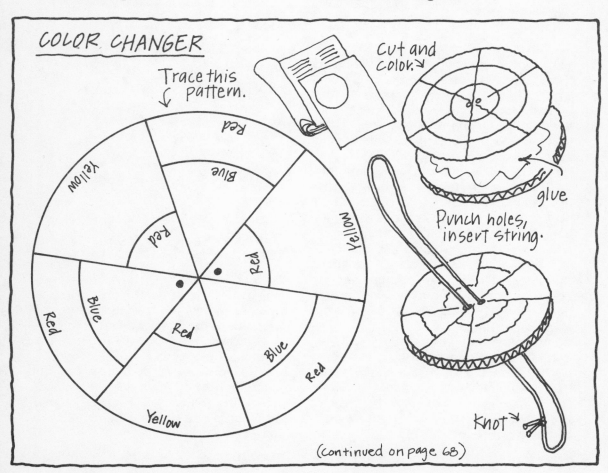

COLOR CHANGER

Trace this pattern.

Cut and color.

glue

Punch holes, insert string.

Knot

(continued on page 68)

7. To spin your changer, center the circle on the string. Twirl it around half a dozen times to put some twists in the string. Pull it tight so the circle unwinds. As it unwinds, relax the string and the motion will cause the string to wind up in the opposite direction. (It's sort of like what happens when you spin around in a swing.)

8. When it finishes winding all the way, give the string a pull to make it unwind.

9. Keep up the pull-relax, wind-unwind motion and your color changer will begin spinning faster and faster.

You know you are doing it right when the colors begin to go strange and it makes a weird wonderful humming noise. Be patient. It may take a bit of time to get the knack.

Did the colors change as you predicted? There are a million different ways to color a changer. Make your own design on the other side. Design it to show every color of the rainbow. Or make one that is black and white and red all over.

MAKE ANOTHER DESIGN ON THE OTHER SIDE.

Color Changer: The Principle of the Thing

Some colors are made from a combination of two other colors. The color changer causes your eye to receive two different color signals from the same place. They go by so fast that your eye doesn't see them as flashes of two colors. Rather it sees two signals from the same spot. Then your brain combines these into one. For example, your brain turns fast flashes of blue and red into purple.

68

Twirlers

When a black cat suddenly becomes a gray streak, you don't get alarmed and think that you're going crazy or that the world is coming to an end. You happen to know that the German shepherd next door is on the loose and that the cat is making a quick getaway. When you turn on a fan and the blades suddenly become a round circle, you don't panic and think the world is going funny. You know they have started spinning. The spinning action has turned the blades into a blur.

Motion has the ability to really change the world around you. When you're speeding down the highway, it turns the dashes down the center of the road into a blurry line. It blends the trees by the side of the road into a smear. It makes a picket fence a tone. Motion can fool your eyes, but your experience keeps your brain from being fooled. Make a twirler and see if you have enough experience to predict how a spinning motion will change a design.

You Will Need
**plastic lids from yogurt or cottage
   cheese pots**
magazine pages
scissors
**a mat knife or a single-edged razor
   blade**
paper
a pencil with an eraser
a pin

1. Trace the outline of the lid onto paper.
2. Cut it out.
3. Fold it in quarters. Open it up. Mark the center spot where the lines cross.
4. Lay it on the lid so it fits exactly.
5. Push a pin through the center to mark the lid.
6. Cut a cross with the mat knife at the center.
7. Push the pencil through the cuts.
8. Twirl the pencil so it spins on its eraser end. Adjust the pencil so you get a good spin.
9. Cut some circles from magazine pages the same size as the lid.
10. Cut crosses in the centers so you can slide the circles over the pencil onto the lid.
11. Slide one circle onto the pencil. Let it rest on the lid. Before you give it a whirl predict what sort of pattern the motion will make.
12. Record your prediction on a chart like the one pictured on the next page.
13. Give it a spin.
14. Record what you actually saw. Do you consider yourself a topnotch predictor?

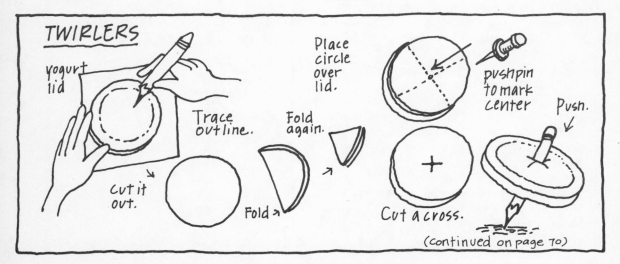

TWIRLERS
yogurt lid
Trace outline.
Cut it out.
Fold
Fold again.
Place circle over lid.
Cut a cross.
pushpin to mark center
Push.

(continued on page 70)

Making Money

There is a way to make money without doing any work, and it's perfectly legal. Turn two cents into three cents. Since the same principle applies to all coins you may as well use quarters, and change fifty cents into seventy-five.

1. Hold two coins, one on top of the other, between your thumb and index finger. Hold them up so they are at eye level.

2. Quickly slide them back and forth across each other.

3. Look at the edges and you will see three coins instead of two.

Unfortunately, this effect lasts only while the coins are in motion. It is unlikely that you will be able to spend the extra money at a store, unless you are pretty quick, or the clerk is pretty slow.

With your knowledge of persistent vision, can you explain where the extra money comes from?

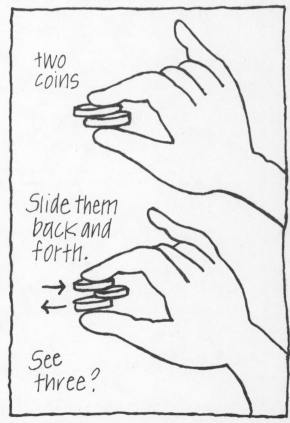

two coins

Slide them back and forth.

See three?

Coming up next:

One-Eyed Crazies:
studying your vision in depth

One-Eyed Crazies

One-Eyed Sights

You have the power to make a pencil jump around while holding it perfectly still. It sounds impossible, but it can be done.

You Will Need
a pencil

1. Hold the pencil out at arm's length.
2. Close one eye and line the point up with something in the distance.
3. While holding the pencil perfectly still, put your free hand over the open eye and look with the other one.
4. Switch back and forth for a really jumpy pencil.

Cover one eye.

Line up the point.

Switch eyes.

It's moving!

If you look carefully, you will notice that you are not seeing exactly the same thing. You actually have two points of view—one from each eye. Almost the same, but slightly different. The pencil occupies a slightly different place in the picture of the world that each eye sees. When you switch back and forth, the pencil's position appears to jump around even though you know that you are holding it still.

Tip Touching

Bet you can't bring the tips of two ordinary pencils together so that they touch. It's easy? Not if you use only one eye. It's just about impossible using only one. Want to give it a try?

Touch tips with two eyes.

Touch tips with one eye.

1. Shut one eye. If you can't wink, make an eye cover with a bandanna.
2. Hold a pair of pencils out at arm's length with your arms spread, one in either hand.
3. Bring them together quickly, aiming to make the points touch. Don't stab yourself.

Was it a hit or a miss? How many tries until you got it right?

Turn a Friend into Twins

If your field of vision were a TV screen, you would get a clear sharp picture on your screen in living color—but only in the center. The rest of the screen would be a fuzzy, blurry, black-and-white, messy, double-image picture. If it were a TV, you'd take it in for repairs in a minute. But you don't because you only watch the center of the screen. Otherwise, you'd have noticed what kind of a weird picture you have been receiving.

Here is an experiment designed to drive your eyes crazy.

1. Ask a friend to stand across the room. A spot with a plain background is best.

2. Hold your finger up in front of you at arm's length, so that you can see both finger and friend.

3. Now focus on the finger. Keep looking at the finger, but at the same time, notice the background.

You should see two fuzzy friends. When this happens you are tempted to bring your friend into focus and check what's going on. The second you do this, you will lose the double image. The trick is to notice it without looking directly at it. The double image is always there then.

Depth Perception

Your conclusions will tell you that seeing things in depth is very difficult using only one eye. Your two eyes work together to keep the world from looking flat.

Both eyes move together, powered by muscles that twist them around in their sockets so that they follow the action.

These muscles send messages to the brain about their movements. When they look at something in the distance, the message to the brain says something like, "Yep, we're looking straight ahead." If a big fat fly lands on your nose, your eyes turn toward your nose. The muscle message to the brain is, "We are turning hard to the inside."

The angles and amounts of turning are recorded in your brain's experience bank. This then estimates how far in the distance something is, based on your experience. In fact, you can feel this happening. Shut your eyes and pretend you are looking off in the distance. Now pretend you are looking at your nose. Even with your eyes shut, you can feel the difference between near and far.

One amazing way that your brain helps you with depth perception occurs when you are walking. Have you ever noticed that when you are approaching a curb on the street, you know well beforehand which foot you will step up with? Without even thinking about it, you have calculated how many steps it is to the curb.

One-Eyed Theater

You are seeing double. Your brain does such a good job of putting the views from your two eyes together that you probably never noticed you were seeing two things at once. The one-eyed theater is a simple device that will give you an in-depth demonstration of your natural ability to look double but see single.

You Will Need
scissors
tape
a couple of objects
a box (cardboard fruit carton)
paper
a pencil

1. First, cut the box in half diagonally, as shown in the illustration below.

2. Cut holes for your eyes. They should be 1 inch apart.

3. Set the theater up on a table. Tape it into position.

4. Draw a line down the center of the floor.

5. Set up objects along the centerline one behind the other (see illustration).

6. Cut a slip of paper big enough to block one eye hole. Tape it into position covering the right eye.

7. Set up a sheet of paper with three squares like the ones in the illustration.

8. Make three drawings. Let one be with the left eye blocked, one with the right eye blocked, one with both eyes open.

9. Compare the views you've drawn on paper.

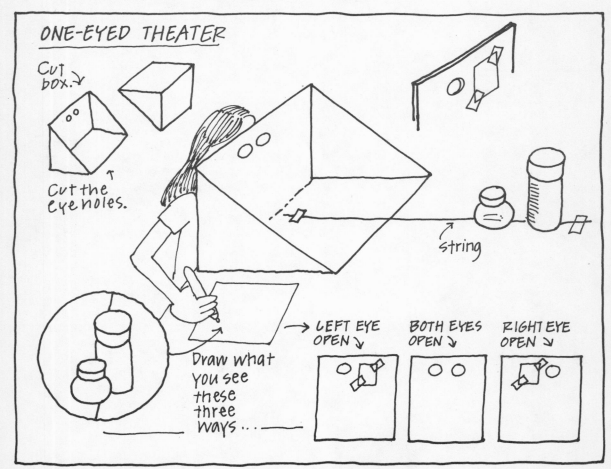

ONE-EYED THEATER

Cut box.

Cut the eye holes.

string

Draw what you see these three ways...

LEFT EYE OPEN

BOTH EYES OPEN

RIGHT EYE OPEN

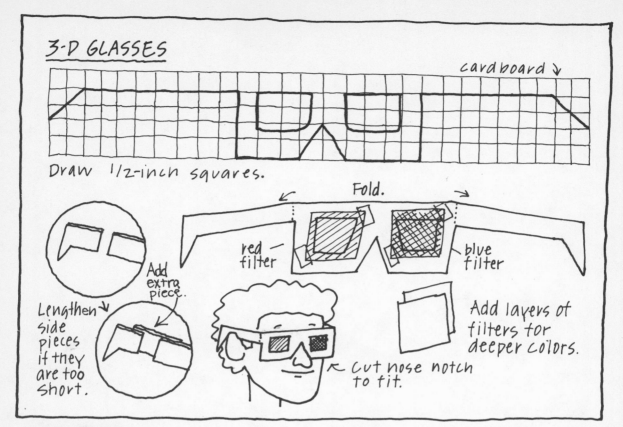

3-D GLASSES

Draw 1/2-inch squares.

cardboard ↓

Fold.

red filter

blue filter

Add extra piece.

Lengthen side pieces if they are too short.

Cut nose notch to fit.

Add layers of filters for deeper colors.

3-D Glasses

See colors vibrate. Watch your drawings jump off the page. Observe dots go dotty and blue come unglued. Get a whole new view of the world with a pair of 3-D glasses. While you are having such a wonderful time with these weird spectacles, you can also learn a bit more about your two-eyed sight system.

You Will Need

lightweight cardboard at least 14 inches long (the back of a legal-size paper pad or a shirt board from the laundry)

scissors

red and blue filter material (colored acetate from an art store)

a pencil

a ruler

tape

1. Cut out a cardboard rectangle that measures 14 inches by 2½ inches.

2. Mark the cardboard off into ½-inch squares.

3. Trace the outline of the glasses from the illustration onto the grid.

4. Cut them out.

5. Try them on. If they don't fit, adjust them by cutting the nose notch a bit bigger or by extending the ear pieces outward with another piece of cardboard.

6. Tape a red filter in one eye.

7. Tape a blue filter in the other eye. The two colors should be about the same intensity (darkness). Use a couple of layers to make them equally dark if you need to.

8. While you are assembling them, predict what you will see when you put them on. Purple? Mostly blue because it's your favorite color?

9. Try them on. Are your predictions correct?

3-D Drawing

To get 3-D effects from your 3-D glasses you need to make some 3-D drawings.

You Will Need
a red pencil
a blue pencil
white paper

1. Draw a red line. Right next to it draw a blue line.

2. Put on your 3-D glasses. Look at the drawing. Watch the colors vibrate.

3. Now pick up your red pencil and draw a cube. Just to the left of each red line, draw a blue line so that you have a blue cube right next to, but not quite touching, the red one.

When you view a red/blue drawing with your glasses on you should see an illusion of depth. The cube will look deeper or more three dimensional than either a plain red or blue cube. (You can compare by putting a hand over your red side, then over the blue one.)

Don't leave your glasses on too long. All that jumping back and forth from red to blue can give you a headache. If your eyes start to hurt, take off your glasses and give your brain a rest.

Sharpen your red and blue pencils and experiment with making different kinds of 3-D drawings. See what makes the best effects. Try touching and crossing the colored lines or leaving a little white space between the two.

Grids, geometrics, and dot drawings all make interesting designs. All parts of your drawing don't have to be 3-D. How about a flat man with weird 3-D eyes? How would you draw someone in deep trouble?

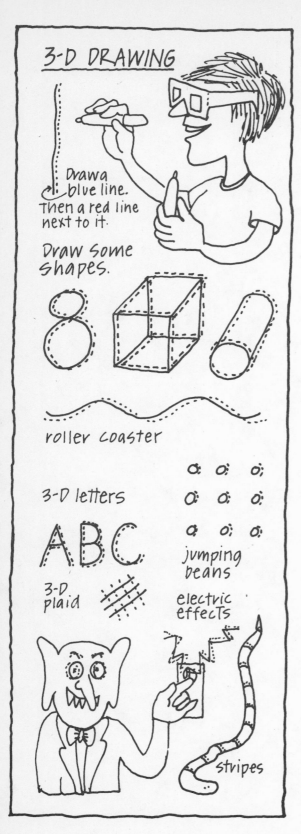

3-D DRAWING

Draw a blue line. Then a red line next to it.

Draw some shapes.

roller coaster

3-D letters

ABC

3-D plaid

jumping beans

electric effects

stripes

3-D: The Principle of the Thing

The winking effect is caused by the fact that one of your eyes is seeing a red image and the other is seeing a blue image. Your brain is trying to put the two views together. It is an impossible job.

Instead, you see red for an instant, then blue for an instant, then red. The quick switching back and forth is what causes the winking. This jumping back and forth creates the same muscular sensations that cause you to see depth.

How do you like my new 3-D suit?

crazy.

Seeing in Depth

For a little more frustrated fun, try threading a needle with one eye. While you are working on that you might think of what else you'd have trouble with if you couldn't perceive depth.

Whether swinging from limb to limb or traveling at high speeds in a car, seeing in depth is important. It helps us get a fix on how fast obstacles are coming up. That way we can cross a street or catch a pop fly. It allows us to either contact or avoid things in our space. Knowing exactly where the barriers and stumbling blocks are is basic to our survival.

3-D Movies

For a while in the 1950s, whole crowds of strangers sat together in large dark rooms, wearing cardboard glasses with one red eye and one blue eye, staring at a screen for hours on end. It was not a strange religion. It was the days of the 3-D movies.

Filmmakers had learned how to splice red and blue images onto film to create exactly the same illusion that you have made with the 3-D glasses. Since they used photography, the effect looked especially real. People screamed in horror (they were mostly horror movies). People got up and ran out of the theater as monsters from outer space attacked the room. Or jet planes flew right at them. Or they took rides on giant roller coasters.

Every once in a while you can catch a rerun of a 3-D film at a theater that shows old movies. Don't miss it!

D for Dimension

The "D" in 3-D stands for dimension; 3-D refers to the third dimension. And what does that mean? To talk about something having dimensions is to talk about how it exists in space. Everything that exists has some kind of dimension.

Pretend for a moment that you are in a car in a parking garage. You are driving down aisles between the rows looking for a place to park. This is a one-dimensional trip: a straight-line journey between two points.

Now when you turn and drive across the parking lot you are traveling in the second dimension. You are on a flat surface. A flat surface is called a "two-dimensional space." Parking lots are not the only thing with two dimensions. Any flat surface is two-dimensional—a sheet of paper or a surface of still water on your fish tank.

When you drive up the ramp in the parking lot to the next level, you are traveling into the third dimension. Now you are not stuck on the surface. You can move up and down as well as side to side in space.

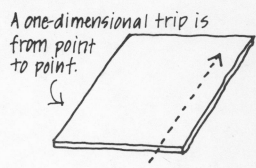

A one-dimensional trip is from point to point.

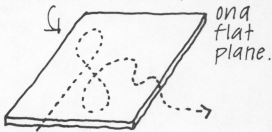

A two-dimensional trip is one that moves in any direction on a flat plane.

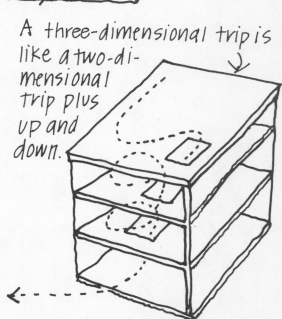

A three-dimensional trip is like a two-dimensional trip plus up and down.

Coming up next:

Making It Big:
making and using magnifiers

Making It Big

Expansion Chamber

Here's an item that will make a marble appear to gain weight, or at least make it swell up in size. Use it to display your favorite cats' eyes and clearies. Or a collection of sea shells or pet rocks. Whatever you place in a biggering jar looks more important. It is not your eyes playing tricks on you. It's a bit of automatic magnification. Where a clear curved object is involved, some magnification is bound to happen.

You Will Need
a bottle
water
bleach
waterproof objects

1. Put your waterproof treasures in a curved glass bottle.
2. Fill it to the top with water.
3. Add a spoonful of bleach to keep wildlife from growing inside.
4. Screw the lid on tight.
5. Now show off your larger-than-life treasures.

Lentils in Your Eye

Lenses are light benders. They are made from glass or other clear materials that have a talent for bending light. There is a lot of science in the shaping of lenses. But basically there are two

EXPANSION CHAMBER

Use these kinds of jars.

olive

jelly

Add a spoonful of bleach.

plastic doodads—
pebbles—
shells

rubber snakes

Screw on lid. →

Display it in a window.

Odd! Every pickle I take out of the jar shrinks.

He's a wizard?

PICKL

Lens, front view

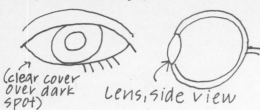

(clear cover over dark spot)

Lens, side view

kinds—the *concave* lens that bends and spreads light out and the *convex* lens that bends and concentrates light in. The word lens comes from the Latin word that means lentil. The Romans (who spoke Latin) noticed that the lens of the human eye looked a lot like a lentil in size and shape. In fact the lens that covers the hole in your eye is a clear material and is designed especially to gather up and bend the light streaming into your eye. It then directs it to the light-sensitive screen at the back (the retina) in a nice orderly way.

Burning Light

Besides bending light, lenses are good for gathering it up and focusing it to a single point. If you've ever fooled around with a magnifying glass (a convex lens), you know how powerful a lens can be. When all the light is pointed toward one spot it becomes very concentrated. It's like having a small portable furnace that gets so hot you can scorch holes in paper.

Magnifiers: The Principle of the Thing

Magnifiers are light benders. When light bounces off the object you are looking at and passes through a magnifying lens, it spreads out (in good order) and takes up more room on the picture screen in your eyeball. As a result, it looks bigger. Scientists call this process magnification. The power of a lens is a measure of how much spreading out of light it can do.

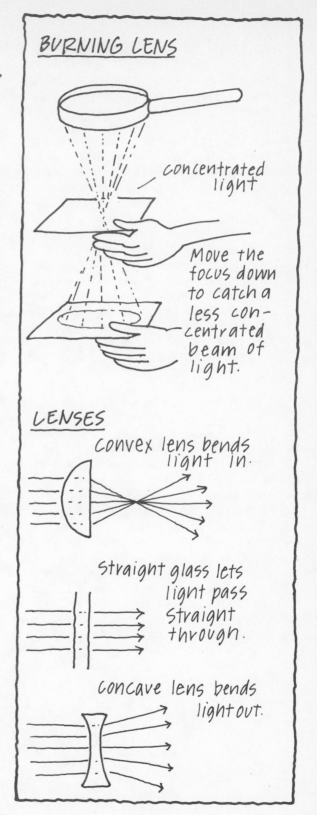

BURNING LENS

concentrated light

Move the focus down to catch a less concentrated beam of light.

LENSES

Convex lens bends light in.

Straight glass lets light pass straight through.

Concave lens bends light out.

Aunt Mary

David's Aunt Mary is a scientist. Not an ancient scientist like Aristotle. Not so famous a scientist as Galileo or Newton. Not yet anyway. But she is getting to be famous because she's figured out how to turn wood into sugar.

Aunt Mary is a modern scientist who goes off to her laboratory every day in Massachusetts to study *Trichoderma reesei* (Try co *der* mah *ree* see i). Mary Mandels is a microbiologist.

Trichoderma is a kind of fungus. (A mushroom is a much larger plant in the fungus family.)

The army asked Mary to study Trichoderma to find a way to control it. This teeny plant had the habit of causing tents to fall apart, clothing to rot, and ropes to break, especially in warm wet places. The army wanted to know how to combat jungle rot.

Mary discovered that when this fungus digests cellulose it turns it into sugar—a trick human stomachs can't do. While jungle rot is not a good thing, sugar is. Why not, she thought, let the fungus make waste wood into something sweet people could eat?

She went back to her lab and began growing fungus in a big way. You could say she became a fungus farmer who is trying to grow the very best wood-eating fungus possible.

The way she does this is to combine the fungus with cellulose. They are kept nice and warm so they grow quickly. The fungus produces a chemical called an enzyme (*en* zime) that breaks down cellulose into sugar. She filters the fungus food mixture to get a pure chemical enzyme. Then she adds more cellulose to the enzyme to make more sugar. The final step is to separate out the sugar in order to find the best strain of fungus and the type of food they prefer.

Mary hopes this process will be able to convert all sorts of waste wood products (and magazines and newspapers) into sugar. In a few years it might be possible. Your cereal box might take a trip to the recycling center and end up back on your breakfast table in your sugar bowl.

Microbiologists

Microbiologists are scientists who often use microscopes. They study the life and behavior of microorganisms (plants and animals that are too small to be seen with the naked eye). They do things like build better sewage treatment plants, work with winemakers, and study how to grow petroleum-eating bacteria to clean up oil spills. A microbiologist would be hard to pick out in a crowd, although they do tend to have squint lines from the long hours they spend peering through microscopes.

Sometimes it's not your size, it's how sharp you are.

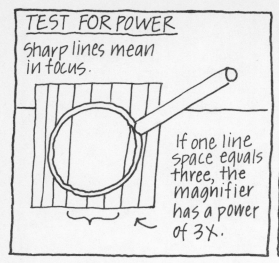

TEST FOR POWER
Sharp lines mean in focus.

If one line space equals three, the magnifier has a power of 3X.

TEST FOR SHARPNESS

Better lenses are sharp all over.

Poorer lenses are sharp only in the middle.

Power Test

Magnifiers are not alike. Some have a lot more power than others (power to spread out light). The more powerful the lens, the bigger it will make things seem.

Are you curious to know how much power you possess? Here is how to measure the magnifying ability of your lens.

You Will Need
paper with lines
a magnifying lens

1. Hold the lens near the lined paper. Move it up and down until you get the lines in focus (looking sharp, not blurry).

2. Compare the number of lines you see outside the lens with the number of lines in the same space that you see through the lens.

If only one line through the magnifier equals three outside, you know the magnifier is making things three times bigger than real life. We say it has a power of three, or 3X.

Power, More or Less?

Having a lot of power isn't always better, not in the magnification busi-

ness. In fact higher powers (anything past about 8X) have some real disadvantages.

When things look a lot bigger, you see a lot less of them. For instance, if you're looking at a bee's legs enlarged 10X, you are likely to see only the bee's knees. There is a danger of getting lost in a forest of hairs and losing track of the big picture—the bee's legs. Also you get a dimmer (less light) view because the area is smaller.

3X, 5X, 8X are good powers for most looking. More important than power is the quality of the lens. It is better to trade power for sharpness any day. It is the sharpness that really lets you see small things clearly.

Test for sharpness with a piece of graph paper (the kind with squares on it). Hold the lens an inch away from your eye and focus on the paper. The less fuzziness and fewer bendy lines you see the better. With the best lenses you will see straight sharp lines from edge to edge, not just in the center.

Scientists often spend thousands of dollars for single lenses that they use to magnify things. Each night before going home, they lock up their lenses just like precious stones. In fact, the lenses are often made out of some very special kinds of glass, sort of like jewels.

How Big Is Small?

How big is something magnified 100 times? How big is the same thing magnified 1,000 times? It's a lot, but how much exactly is hard to imagine. Numbers have a way of meaning nothing at all unless you have a meaty comparison to sink your teeth into.

For instance, imagine a fly. If you could imagine it 1,000 times larger than real life, it would be the size of a small foreign car. To get more of an idea of magnifying something small consider the period at the end of this sentence.

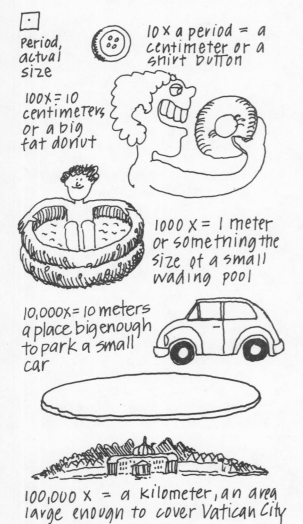

Period, actual size

10 X a period = a centimeter or a shirt button

100X = 10 centimeters or a big fat donut

1000 X = 1 meter or something the size of a small wading pool

10,000X = 10 meters a place big enough to park a small car

100,000 X = a kilometer, an area large enough to cover Vatican City

Blowing Up Things

Imagine a giant fly is buzzing over your bed. Or a monster mealworm. Or an enormous earwig. Or a tremendous toad. With pen and paper magnification you can blow things up to giant, poster size. The secret is the grid. It lets you draw things out-sized while keeping everything in proportion, so it looks right when you finish.

You Will Need
a drawing or photo of something you want to make really big
pencils
a ruler
a big piece of paper

1. It is best to work with a picture of something you want to enlarge. Magazines are good places to find pictures to enlarge.

2. Fold the picture in half and half again. Open it up flat. It should have four equal folds.

3. Make the same folds in the opposite direction.

4. Cut a piece of paper the size you want the poster to be. Make sure it is the same proportion (shape) as the original picture.

5. Mark off the poster paper into a 16-section grid pattern like the one on the picture. Use a ruler and light pencil lines to do this.

6. Draw the outline of the subject onto the big paper. The trick is to forget the big picture and transfer the outline one square at a time.

7. The big picture will take shape automatically. And it will look right in proportion.

8. Go over the drawing in ink. Erase the pencil lines. Fill in the details.

How many times bigger do you want the poster to be? Twice as big? Then make the edge of the poster two times bigger than the edge of the original picture. Three times? Then the poster edge should be three times bigger.

BLOWING UP THINGS

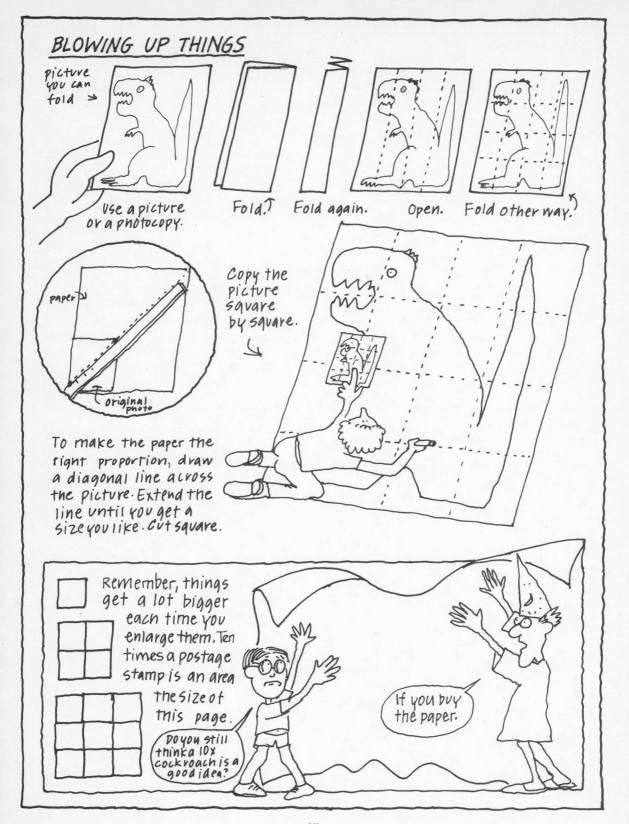

picture you can fold →

Use a picture or a photocopy.

Fold. Fold again. Open. Fold other way.

paper

original photo

Copy the picture square by square.

To make the paper the right proportion, draw a diagonal line across the picture. Extend the line until you get a size you like. Cut square.

Remember, things get a lot bigger each time you enlarge them. Ten times a postage stamp is an area the size of this page.

Do you still think a 10x cockroach is a good idea?

If you buy the paper.

Magnifying Simply

Water, wire, and a nail are all that it takes to get you started looking into the world of smallness. Believe it or not a magnifying lens can be made with this simple stuff. The wire gives the water drop something to sit on, while a drop's clear curved surface does the magnifying.

You Will Need
a piece of flexible wire (like copper)
a nail
water

1. Cut a piece of wire 10 inches long.
2. Bend it in half.
3. Slide the nail into the bend.
4. Hold the wire ends with one hand. Twist the nail around with the other to make a loop.
5. Remove the nail. Try to make the loop as round as possible.
6. Carefully put a water drop on the loop with an eyedropper.
7. To use the magnifier, hold it over whatever you want to look at.

Try looking at printing from the newspaper for starters. Find a printed word. Move the magnifier closer and farther away from the word until the writing becomes clear and sharp.

A holder for the magnifier will keep your hands free while you are looking. Drive the nail into a block of wood so it stands straight. Bend the handle of the magnifier around the nail to hold it in place.

Another way to put the magnifying power of a water drop to work is to carefully place one on a clear sheet of glass. The drop naturally takes on the round shape of a lens. Move it into position over the specimen you want to see. Look through the drop at the subject you are viewing.

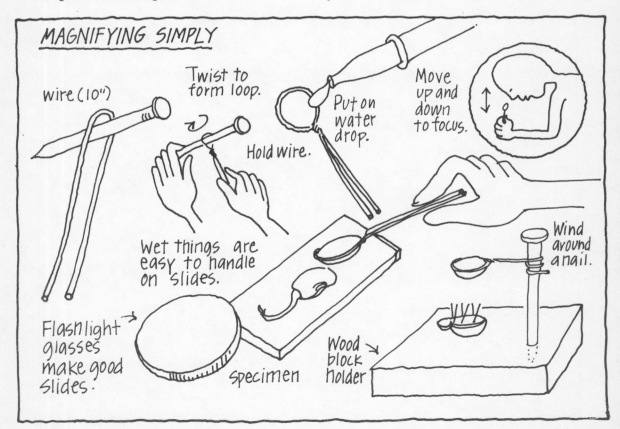

MAGNIFYING SIMPLY

wire (10")

Twist to form loop.

Hold wire.

Put on water drop.

Move up and down to focus.

Wet things are easy to handle on slides.

Wind around a nail.

Flashlight glasses make good slides.

Specimen

Wood block holder

Little Wonders

Lucky for you you don't see all small things. For instance, a look at your hands just after you have finished washing them will surprise you. Look at those fingertip nooks and crannies with a magnifying lens and you'll find a shocking amount of dirt and debris. If you want to be really grossed out, take a closer look with a magnifier at what might be wedged under your toenails. Not all close observations will be quite so horrifying. There are many fascinating discoveries to be made by looking at the little things around your house.

Magnifying History

Over 300 years ago, a man named Anton van Leeuwenhoek had a theory about pepper. He thought that the reason it felt hot in the mouth was because it was covered with teeny barbs. Inside the mouth it would prick and scrape your tongue and cause a burning, hot sensation. His way of testing his theory was to look closely. Closer than anyone had looked at pepper before.

He did this with the aid of a tiny glass bubble—a lens—that he made himself. He wasn't the first person to look through a lens. It was common knowledge that lenses made little things look bigger. He just did it better than anyone had ever done it before. Grinding lenses was his hobby, though his job was being a janitor. It was a hobby he pursued with great enthusiasm. His little lenses were so carefully made that he could magnify things with a sharpness that had never been possible before. With his little lenses he was able to see things 200 times bigger than their actual size.

It is not certain whether he ever discovered the hot secrets of peppercorns,

MAGNIFIERS

You might want to try using a more powerful lens than the water drop microscope. You can buy magnifiers from different kinds of stores.

3x reading glass (dime store)

40x pocket microscope

8x (photo store)

(science supply store)

multi-lens 3x, 5x, 8x (science supplier)

2x bug box (toy store)

TRY LOOKING AT:

sprouts

molds

thin slice of cork

feathers

instant coffee

ALSO TRY:

Peach fuzz, fish scales, taste buds, dust, hairs, crystals (salt, sugar, alum), rust, insects, plant parts.

but his lens revealed that they were smooth on the surface.

Whole new worlds opened up as he turned his little lenses on bits of meat, seeds, hairs, the gunk on teeth. He saw blood cells moving through the finer-than-hair capillaries in living tissue. He saw single cells. He found tiny animals swimming, living, and dying in a drop of pond water.

The devices he looked through were called microscopes. The microscopes he used were a lot different from the complicated contraptions that modern scientists use. They were tiny rounded pieces of glass (some about 1/8 inch across) mounted in metal rectangles. His method was to make a microscope and attach a subject under it—for months, or permanently. He would study something for hours, then make careful drawings and notes of what he saw.

When he wasn't grinding or drawing, he wrote letters. A lot of letters. He sent more than 400 letters (or papers, as scientists call them) to the French Academy of Science and the Royal Society of England.

You can imagine what the French and English scientists thought when they first received these wild reports from a Dutch janitor about invisible animals in their drinking water. They were skeptical, to say the least. They kept their eyebrows up until 1677. That is when Robert Hooke, a famous English scientist, made a microscope according to the instructions that the crazy janitor had written. To Hooke's amazement everything van Leeuwenhoek had said was true. After this, van Leeuwenhoek made a gift of the lenses to the fellows of the Royal Society so they could look for themselves. They were so amazed and impressed at what he had discovered that they made him a member of their society.

During his life he made more than 400 microscopes and wrote more than 400 papers which told of his amazing discoveries. Kings and queens came to his home in the town of Delft to peer through his microscopes.

Anton van Leeuwenhoek is remembered today for opening up the unexplored territory of the microworld and discovering new life forms. He is given credit for beginning the science of biology. Quite amazing, considering all this was accomplished as a hobby by a janitor who never left his home town.

Looking Alike

Symmetry

Symmetry is a word scientists and artists use to describe something that has sameness (or parts that are alike) on different sides. If you cut the smirror design on the next page in half, you get two parts that are the same. It has two-sided sameness, or symmetry. You could also call it *bilaterally* (bi *lat* er al lee) *symmetrical*. Which is the scientific word for two-sided sameness.

Sameness doesn't just take sides. It can be found arranged around a point in the center; this is called *radial* (round) *symmetry*. Or in a line like a picket fence. Then it's called *sliding symmetry*. Question: What kind of symmetry does a baseball have? A nose?

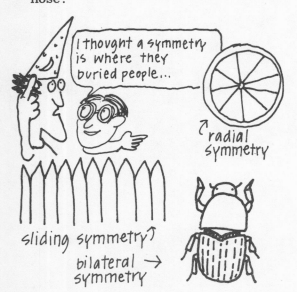

I thought a symmetry is where they buried people...

radial symmetry

sliding symmetry

bilateral symmetry

Asymmetry

You may get the feeling that everything is symmetrical. There is a lot of it around. But there are plenty of things that aren't.

These things also have a special name. They are *asymmetrical*.

Some things, such as your ear, are just plain odd-shaped. They don't even come close to being symmetrical. Then there are things that are almost symmetrical, but something within their design kills their symmetry. Imagine a person with a wooden leg or an all-white dog with one black spot.

Asymmetry looks like this.

Smirror Painting

Blob art. Squash drawings. Fold-and-smash pictures. This project could be called a lot of things. Perhaps you have done this project before, under a different name. What you might not have known is that besides making some nifty patterns, it makes a special kind of design. A symmetrical design.

You Will Need
paint (a thick kind, poster paint works best)
paper
newspaper
brushes
bottles (like squeeze detergent bottles)

1. Put down a layer of newspaper to work on. The squash process can be a bit messy.

2. Mix up at least two colors of paint. Make it thick.

3. Fold the paper in half. Open it up.

4. Squirt, brush, or drop paint on the paper on only one side of the fold.

5. Fold the paper closed and press out the blobs with your hands.

6. Open it and admire your bilaterally symmetrical art work.

You can control the design by directing the paint as you press out the blobs.

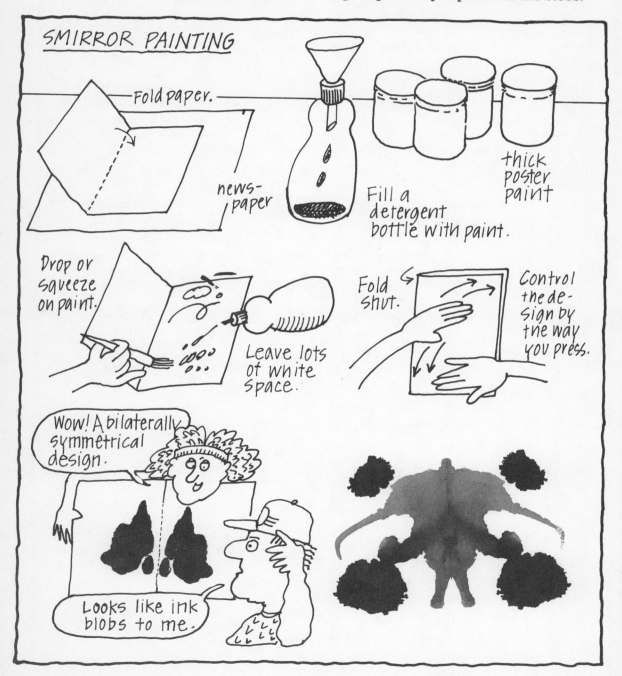

Symmetry Tester

Want to see a symmetry detector? It's nothing but a mirror? True, but did you know that another way to describe something symmetrical is to say one side is the mirror image of the other? If you suspect something is symmetrical you can test it by putting the mirror down along the *axis of symmetry,* or dividing line. That's the imaginary line dividing the parts that are the same. If the design looks the same in the mirror, you've got it, a genuine example of *bilateral* (two-sided) *symmetry.*

**You Will Need
a flat-sided mirror**

1. Predict whether or not the thing is symmetrical.

2. Put the mirror along the axis of symmetry.

3. If the thing looks the same in real life as it does in the reflection, it's symmetrical.

Don't stop testing too quickly. Sometimes a thing can have two axes of symmetry or three. Or more. Symmetry can show up in all sorts of different shapes.

You need a mirror that has a flat side. If you can't find one at home, you can buy one for not very much money at a dime store or a drugstore, in the cosmetics department. A piece of shiny silver Mylar or heavy aluminum foil mounted on a cardboard back will make a satisfactory substitute.

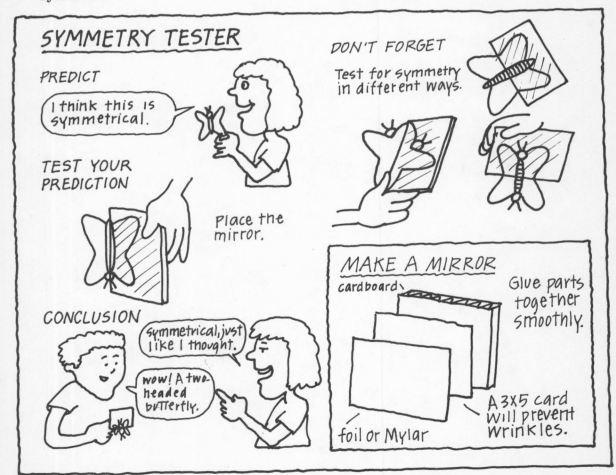

SYMMETRY TESTER

PREDICT

I think this is symmetrical.

TEST YOUR PREDICTION

Place the mirror.

CONCLUSION

Symmetrical, just like I thought.

Wow! A two-headed butterfly.

DON'T FORGET

Test for symmetry in different ways.

MAKE A MIRROR

cardboard

Glue parts together smoothly.

A 3X5 card will prevent wrinkles.

foil or Mylar

Symmetrical or Not?

Try these things with your symmetry detector. First predict, then test. Are these examples bilateral, radial, rotational, or asymmetrical? Where is the axis of symmetry? The answers are in The Back of the Book.

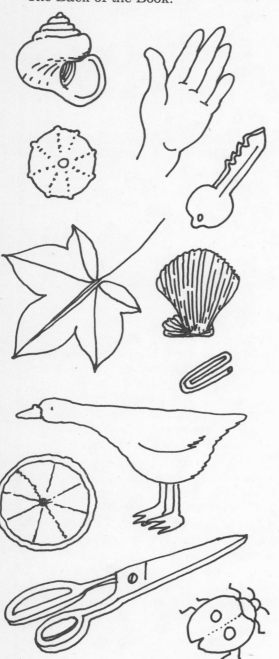

Stalking the Wild Symmetry

How about taking your symmetry detector outdoors and looking for some wild symmetry? By now you shouldn't need it. You should be able to spot symmetry a mile away. But if you're not sure, you can check with your detector.

Make it a game. Find friends who are also expert in symmetry, and challenge them to a duel. Make it a race to discover the most symmetries. You will need to set some limits in time and territory. Also decide whether you will bring back the actual real live symmetries, or if a drawing or list will do. Of course, you can invent more rules to make the hunt more interesting. How about blue-eyed, bilateral symmetries only? Or biological, brown symmetries? Ready? Set? Start stalking wild symmetries.

Two-Faced You

Would you say your face is symmetrical? Get a photo of yourself. It must be a full-face photo (one that is taken with you looking straight at the camera). Put a straight-sided mirror down along the midpoint to test for symmetry. How do you look? Weird? Try the other side. Does it look a bit weird too?

A normal face is a little different on each side. Different enough to make you look weird if you suddenly started wearing either side of your face twice. Have you ever heard of actors wanting to be photographed only on their best side? Now you know what they meant. Do you have a side you like best? And while you're taking sides, do you still think you would call your face symmetrical?

Mirror Image

Fold a sheet of paper. Cut out a heart. Both sides are the same, right?

Now cut it along the fold. Slide one side so it sits on top of the other. It isn't the same is it? It won't be the same until you give it a twist and flip it over. When it's reversed, it fits perfectly.

In mirror images, both sides are exactly the same but with one big difference. One side is a flopped over, backwards reflection of the other.

Mirrors are not the only place you will find mirror images. There are lots of them to stumble over in real life—your own two feet, for instance. And your shoes are a perfect example of being alike in every respect—except one is a backwards, or mirror, version of the other. Hands and gloves are good examples too.

Making Mutants

Ever look into a mirror and see somebody looking back with four eyes? Or two mouths? Have you ever seen a mirror that has the power to turn just about anything into an interesting and sometimes horrifying design?

All you need is a mirror with a flat side and some things to test. Pictures in magazines are good. Try testing a face for symmetry. First, fool around with the mouth, shifting the axis of symmetry, making it thinner or wider. For more startling changes move the mirror to make a face with two mouths, four eyes, and two bottom lips.

Automatic Two-Sided Drawing

Imagine a kind of drawing where you do only half the work. The other half is automatic and an exact reversed replica of the first. Draw a complicated design. Invent an animal, a snake, a face, or a place with automatic symmetry.

You Will Need
thin, thirsty paper (tissue, napkins, or paper towels will work)
juicy felt markers

1. Press the paper flat.

2. Fold it in half.

3. Draw half of a design. Remember the fold will be the center line. (Think of the fold as the axis of symmetry.)

4. Open it up. Touch up the outline with a marker if parts are missing.

5. Color the design with colored markers.

Be careful not to tear the thin paper as you work.

Draw a face using the automatic method. Or a two-headed mutant with one eye. Or Siamese twins. Design some bilateral animal bodies or some very complicated designs.

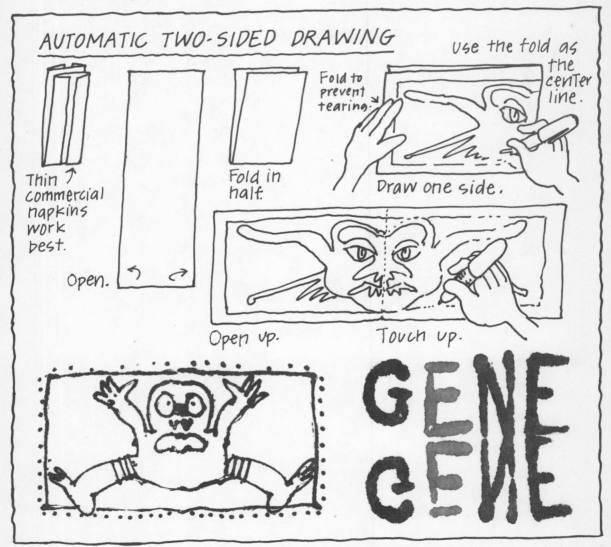

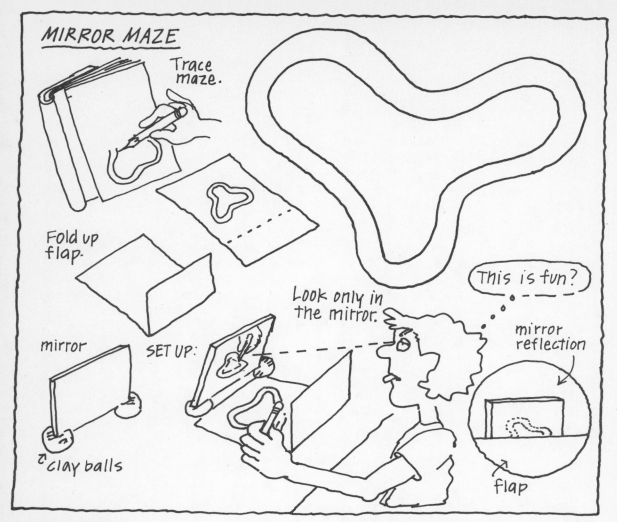

Mirror Maze

Want to feel frustrated? Out of control? Uncoordinated, like a real klutz? You already do? Well, this experiment will give you an excuse. It will also give you more opportunity to find out about the peculiar habits of mirrors.

You Will Need
a mirror
some clay balls
a pencil
paper (not too heavy)

1. Put the paper down flat over the maze drawing. If you can't trace the maze you need to find some thinner paper.

2. Trace the maze drawing onto the paper.

3. Fold the end up to make a wall.

4. Stand the mirror up by pressing its corners into two balls of clay. Adjust it so you can see the maze and your hand holding the pencil in the mirror, but not directly.

5. Now, looking *only in the mirror,* trace your way around the maze. (A warning: this may look like the world's easiest maze, but it's not. It's amazingly difficult.)

No, you haven't lost your mind. There is something about the mirror that makes this difficult. Can you describe what it is?

Mirror Writing

For a little more frustrating fun, try mirror writing. With the same mirror and paper setup, try writing your name on a paper while looking only in the mirror. No fair peeking. Go slowly and write it so it reads correctly in the mirror. When you're done, check to see what happened. Do the letters change? Which ones don't? Why?

Betcha Can't

So you've mastered mirror writing. You're ready for the ultimate challenge. Try writing upside down, backwards, and laterally inverted (mirror style), while someone dictates. Use both hands and a blindfold. When you master that, try adding both feet to the act.

Secret Mirror Code

A mirror can be a small portable device for decoding messages. Give your best friend a mirror decoder and a code card. All your private communications will be safe from prying eyes.

There are two ways to do this. One way is to write all your messages in a mirror. This method takes longer but after a while, you will be able to do this with ease. Honest. The other way is to go through the alphabet, letter by letter, to make a code card. Do this by writing each letter as it appears in the mirror. Then copy the letters from the card to write a message. Give the message to your friend. It can be decoded by reading it in a mirror.

Private Language

Interested in a really strange and secret code? Develop your own alphabet with new symmetrical symbols for each letter. For instance, the first couple of letters might look like this:

The way to do this is to move the mirror to the letter and draw a shape that you see in the mirror. Of course, there are a lot of ways to do this, so your private code can be unique. Move the mirror around until you get a new letter shape you like. Do this for each letter.

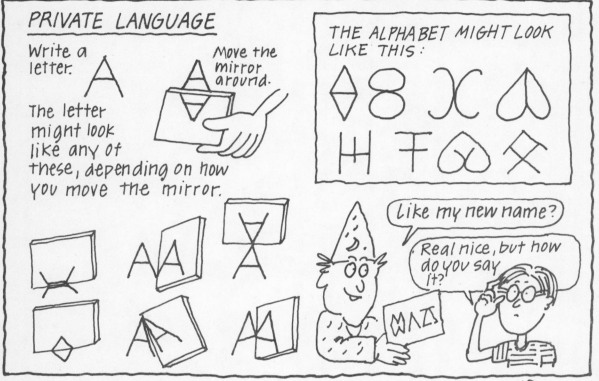

A Name Game

It is just possible that you have a symmetrical name. It's rare, but not unheard of. If you don't there is a good chance you'll find some numbers, symbols, or secret words hidden away in your name. Find out by sliding the mirror along the center of your name and drawing what you see. Don't forget to try this on the lower case and upper case letters of your name. Write your name in all capitals as well as upper- and lowercase letters. Then try script for a variation.

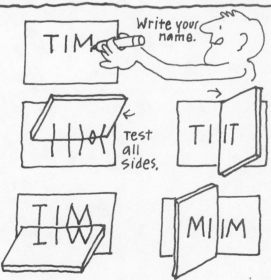

Bet you picked me for mirror drawing because I'm so bright and reflective.

Not exactly.

Mirror Drawing

No matter what you want, they want to do the opposite. Know anybody like that? If so, you're in luck. That person is a perfect partner for mirror drawing. This is the project where one of you is the leader and the other acts like a mirror. The results are hypnotic. Plus you end up with a bonus of big squiggly pages of interesting mirror designs.

You Will Need
a partner
two pens or markers
a big sheet of paper

1. Decide who will be the leader and who will be the mirror.
2. Fold the paper into four sections to help keep track of where you are.
3. Put your pens down somewhere on the opposite but equal spots on the paper.
4. The leader draws slowly. The mirror partner mirrors the action in the opposite direction. If the leader goes right, the mirror goes left, keeping the same shape only reversing the direction. Go slowly, take your time, and have fun.
5. Switch places.
You don't have to stay on your side of the territory. You can cross and double back and curve and turn the corners and—anything you like. Advanced mirror artists might try drawing so they reverse the motion top to bottom *and* left to right, like a real mirror.

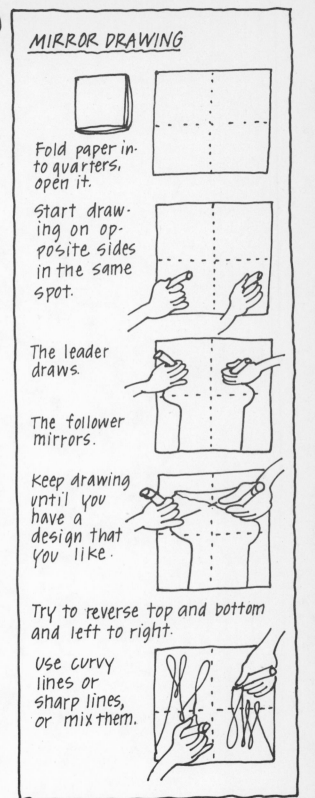

MIRROR DRAWING

Fold paper into quarters, open it.

Start drawing on opposite sides in the same spot.

The leader draws.

The follower mirrors.

Keep drawing until you have a design that you like.

Try to reverse top and bottom and left to right.

Use curvy lines or sharp lines, or mix them.

Balancing the Impossible

Mobiles, Equilibrium on a String

A mobile is a balancing act hung from a string. It is also a kind of sculpture that is delicately balanced and is able to be pushed around by tiny air currents. It's fun to make and fun to watch. Hang it in your room. Let the drafts entertain you.

You Will Need
four plastic straws
string or yarn
scissors
five orange juice can lids
a hammer
a nail
a block of wood

1. Cut nine strings 12 inches long.
2. Knot each string so it forms a loop.
3. Cut slits ¼ inch long into both ends of each straw. Put both slits in the same position.
4. Loop the strings through the holes of each lid (see illustration).
5. To assemble the mobile, start with the straw with two lids. Loop a support string around the midpoint. Make it balance.
6. Slip the support string into the slit of the next straw. Loop a support string around the center. Predict where it will balance. Then slide it back and forth until you find the point where it balances when the straw is level with the floor.

7. Slip the support string into the slit of the next straw.
8. Add the rest of the straws in the same way.
9. Hang the whole thing by the last string from the ceiling in your room.
Watch balance at work.

Pointed Predictions

You can make a game of predicting the balance points. Guess. Then test your prediction on your finger. If you missed, you have to shift it a bit in one direction or the other. Can you find any pattern in the balance points? If you're not sure, measure the distances from the end of a straw to the spot where the string balances.

How is a mobile like a seesaw?

Your mobile doesn't have to balance horizontally. Here are some other shapes your mobile can take by shifting the balance points a bit.

MOBILE

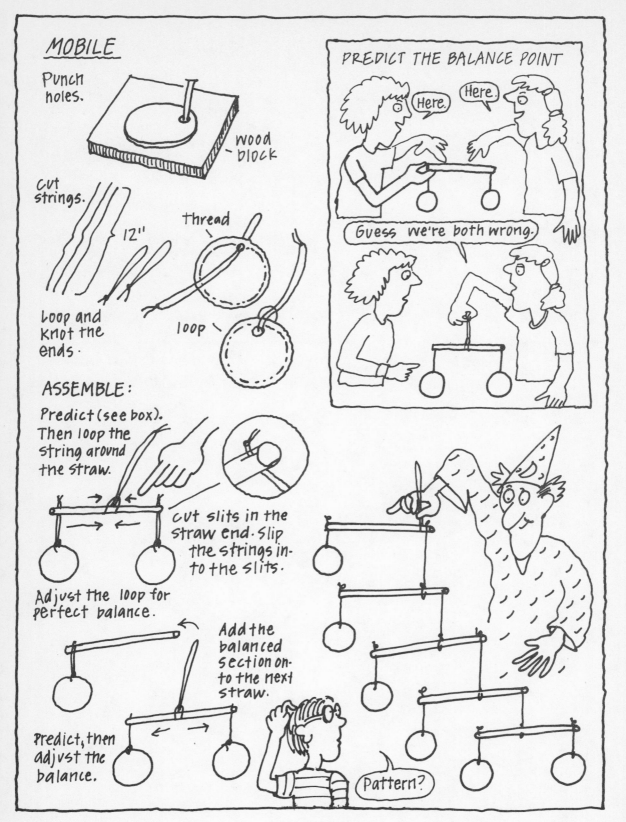

Punch holes.

— WOOD BLOCK

Cut strings.

12"

Loop and knot the ends.

thread

loop

ASSEMBLE:

Predict (see box). Then loop the string around the straw.

Cut slits in the straw end. Slip the strings into the slits.

Adjust the loop for perfect balance.

Add the balanced section onto the next straw.

Predict, then adjust the balance.

PREDICT THE BALANCE POINT

Here. Here.

Guess we're both wrong.

Pattern?

103

Fooling Around with Forks

You may not know how to spell the word physics, but you already know a lot about it. At least the physics of balance. After all, you've spent a lifetime getting the feel of physics. Prove it to yourself. All you need is a pencil and a lump of clay.

1. Find the balance point in this pencil.

2. Roll up a ball of clay. Stick it on the end of the pencil. Now where is the balance point? It moves, right? You probably even knew which way it moved without even testing. (See, you already know quite a lot about physics.)

3. Stand the pencil on its eraser end. Try to balance it. Can you figure out where the center of balance is now?

The reason your hand is wriggling around it is that you are trying to keep the support point under the center of mass (center of gravity). Tricky, isn't it? Unless you know the fork trick.

4. Stick a pair of forks into the clay ball on opposite sides. Make them the same size—in the interest of balance. Fool around adjusting them until you get this weird contraption to balance on your finger.

The forks move the center of mass in a way that lets the pencil stay balanced. See how many positions you can make the flying fork contraption balance in. Often, adding mass to an object makes it easier to balance.

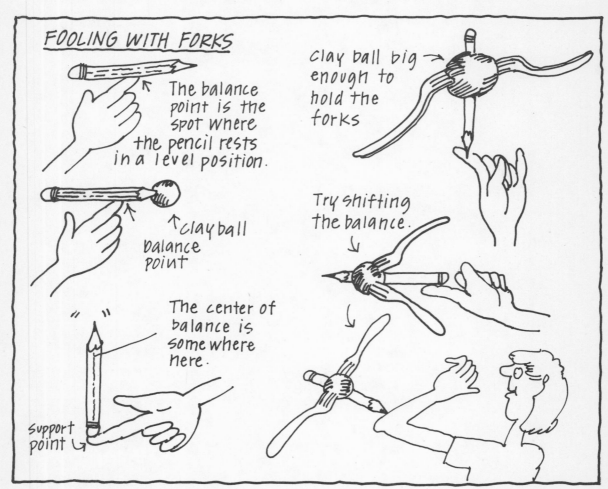

FOOLING WITH FORKS

The balance point is the spot where the pencil rests in a level position.

↑ clay ball balance point

Clay ball big enough to hold the forks

The center of balance is somewhere here.

Support point ↳

Try shifting the balance.

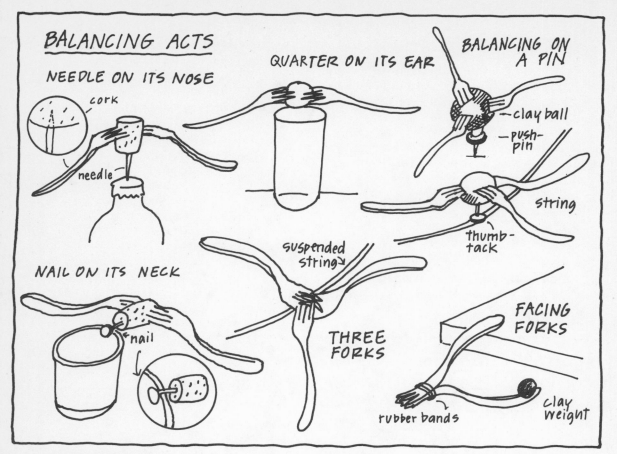

BALANCING ACTS

NEEDLE ON ITS NOSE

cork

needle

NAIL ON ITS NECK

nail

QUARTER ON ITS EAR

suspended string

THREE FORKS

BALANCING ON A PIN

clay ball

push-pin

string

thumb-tack

FACING FORKS

rubber bands

clay weight

Balancing Acts

Here are some balancing stunts that seem to defy the laws of gravity. Indeed, some do, but can you tell which ones? Look them over and guess which ones will. Then check your prediction by making an actual test try. You can amaze your friends and astound your family with the results of your research.

Whatcha doing, wiz?

Testing, testing.

Balance

Balance is what happens when the forces pushing and pulling on an object are such that the object stays still (or at rest). Scientists sometimes call the state of being balanced *equilibrium*.

Mass is matter, or substance with weight. The *center of mass* of an object is a single point where the effect of all the forces pushing and pulling on the object (especially gravity) can be imagined to act. It's where the weight of an object seems to center. The *center of mass* and the *center of gravity* are not exactly the same. But very, very close. Balance point is another word for the center of gravity.

We say something is *balanced* when the support point rests directly under the center of mass.

Certain Center

Ever need to get to the heart of something? What if the something is odd in shape, like a pizza with some big bites out of one side?

You can find its center with this clever detector. It will work on any funny shape, as long as it is flat. Use it to zero in on the center of any odd shape.

You Will Need
lightweight cardboard
string
a pin
a weight (a washer will do)

1. To make the detector, cut a length of string. Tie something heavy, like a washer, on the end.

2. Cut out a weird cardboard shape.

3. To operate the detector, put dots in three different spots on the shape.

4. Push the pin through one of the dots and stick the shape to the wall. Make the pin hole extra big so the shape hangs free.

5. Wind the string around the pin so that the weight hangs straight.

6. Trace a line on the shape along the string. A ruler will help you do this.

7. Do the same for the other two dots.

8. The third line should intersect the other two at the same point. This is the center of the shape.

9. Test your work by balancing the shape where the lines cross on the eraser of a pencil.

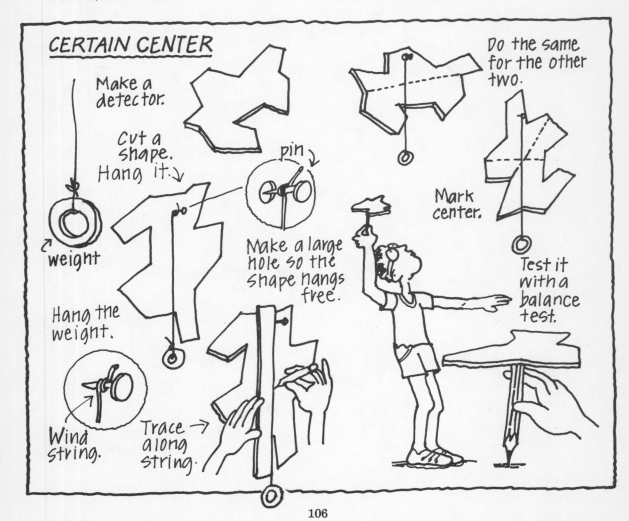

CERTAIN CENTER

Make a detector.

Cut a shape. Hang it. ↓

weight

Hang the weight.

Wind string.

pin

Make a large hole so the shape hangs free.

Trace → along string.

Do the same for the other two.

Mark center.

Test it with a balance test.

Kansas, Easy as Pie

Kids from Kansas live in a nice regular-shaped state. Making a prediction about the center of their state should be a piece of cake. Predicting the center of mass of any regular shape is easy. It will be where it looks like it should be, in the middle. However, finding the center of an irregular shape is difficult. It's hard to guess how the masses fall. If you don't believe it, try searching out centers of odd-shaped states like Florida or California by guesswork.

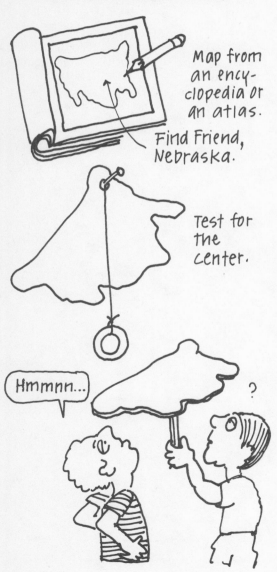

Map from an encyclopedia or an atlas.

Find Friend, Nebraska.

Test for the center.

Hmmnn...

?

True Friend?

Friend, Nebraska, has the reputation of being smack dab in the center of the entire USA. You can even buy a postcard that says, "Write a Friend from Friend." Find out if the folks from Friend are telling the truth about being right at the heart of America.

You Will Need
a center detector
cardboard
glue
a map of the USA or one to trace

1. Trace the map of the USA onto a sheet of paper.
2. Glue it to some cardboard.
3. Cut it out.
4. Test it with your center detector.

Well, are the folks from Friend telling the truth?

Any predictions about where the midpoint in your state might be?

Comeback Can

It is pretty easy to guess at the center of mass because it looks like it's at the center of things. But when it changes its location, weird things can happen, or appear to happen. You can use the force of gravity and some secret mass to create motion that will baffle your friends.

You Will Need
a large cake tin with a lid (like the kind
  fruit cakes come in)
a magnet or metal ounce weights
  (something like keys will work)
tape

1. Stick the metal object to the inside wall of the tin. Three keys taped to the side works fine.

2. Put the lid on tight. Your comeback can is ready.

3. Hold the can so the weight is at the top only slightly forward. Secretly mark the spot that needs to be on top.

4. Let it go so it rolls forward.

5. When it gets close to making a full turn, the can will stop and magically return to your hand.

If you want to use the comeback can as a magic trick, make up a wild story about how certain kinds of metal have special attractive forces or the ability to return like homing pigeons. Then set the can up before your audience. Explain it has such mysterious powers. That even if you push it, it will always return.

The can is more responsive if you give it a little forward push. Don't push too hard or your can will roll away, never to return. Your reputation as a magician will suffer.

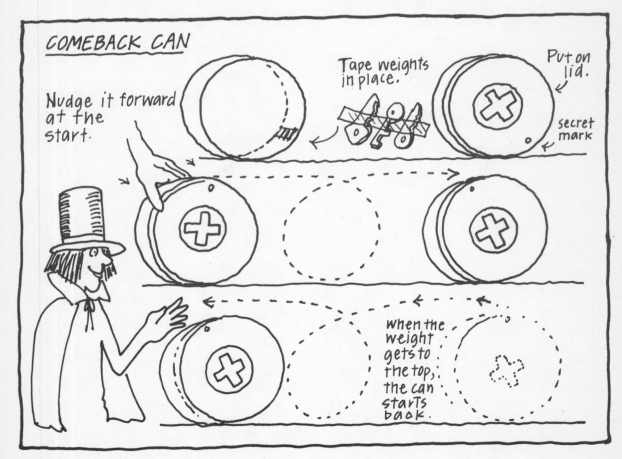

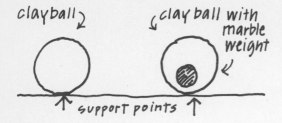

clay ball

clay ball with marble weight

support points

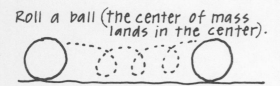

Roll a ball (the center of mass lands in the center).

Roll a ball with a marble weight (more mass). It lands with more mass on the bottom.

A Massive Attraction

You can't always put your finger on the center of mass. In a clay ball, the center of mass is somewhere in the center of the hunk of clay. The *support point* is the spot on which the mass rests.

If you bury a heavy marble in the clay ball you will change its center of mass. The ball with the marble will begin to roll in a funny, wobbly, unbalanced way. It will come to rest with the marble on the bottom. The reason is that the attractive force of gravity pulls more strongly on the more massive side.

Mass Is on a Downer

Given the opportunity, mass likes to get as low as it can go. We are in a constant tug of war with the forces of gravity, because gravity is forever pulling things toward the center of the earth.

One way to describe it is to say that mass is always on a downer. Things tend to come to rest in the most stable position, with the most mass as low as it can go.

3-D Foolers

This is also true for things that are three-dimensional (not flat like cardboard). You have run into something like this if you have ever seen a baby cup. It has extra weight on the bottom,

weighted baby cups

mass

comeback punching bag

weight on the bottom

loaded dice

like one of those balloon punching bags with a weight on the bottom. When you give it a whack, you expect it to stay knocked down, but the weight at the bottom causes it to roll right back up again. The extra weight in the bottom of the hull of a sailboat works the same way—it helps to stabilize the boat in rough water.

Do You Dare?

It is very easy to make it absolutely impossible for a person to get out of a chair. No glue. No ropes. No nothing. Here's how to do it.

You Will Need
an armless straight-backed chair
a victim
a dollar (optional)

1. Have your friend sit down.
2. Tell her you will bet her a dollar (more if you have found a real sucker) that she will be unable to get up without using her hands or leaning forward. Also, her feet should be flat on the floor.

Go ahead, bet as much as you want — your money is safe. There is no way the person can get out of that chair. Try it and see.

If your friend liked being helpless in a chair, she or another friend might enjoy being stuck to the floor or up against the wall or unable to lift a foot. Here are more awkward tricks to test your friend's equilibrium. And yours.

Dare You to Unglue One Shoe. For this stunt you need a wall. Stand so the left side of your whole body rests along one wall. Make sure the left foot, hip and cheek are touching the wall. Now, dare you to lift the right foot off the floor.

Dare You to Lift the Dollar. For this stunt you need a dollar, a wall, and a friend with a dollar. (If your friend is the betting kind, his dollar will be yours.) The friend should stand with feet together, both heels against the wall. Set the dollar 12 inches away from the friend's toes. The dollar is his if he can pick it up without moving his feet or bending his knees.

Dare You to Keep on Your Toes. For this stunt bend over and grip your toes. Keep your knees slightly bent. Now hop on your toes.

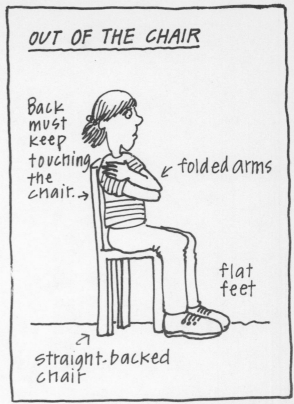

OUT OF THE CHAIR

Back must keep touching the chair. →

← folded arms

flat feet

↗ straight-backed chair

UNGLUE ONE SHOE

left cheek and left foot touching the wall

← Lift this foot from the floor.

110

LIFT THE DOLLAR

so near and yet so far...

no bent knees

feet together

heels touching the wall

ON YOUR TOES

slightly bent knees

Hop?

← Grab toes.

Always in Equilibrium

The reason why a body can't get out of the chair is that it needs to lean forward to do this. (And that's against the rules.) You need to shift your center of gravity to move.

You may have never noticed it before, but your center of balance is constantly shifting. No reason you should have noticed. It is automatically monitored in that amazing computer center in your head: the brain. As you run, jump, skip, walk, or make any move, you really throw your weight around. Your brain makes sure that your body parts take positions that keep you balanced or constantly in equilibrium. Your brain does such a good job of keeping track of your dynamic (constantly shifting) balance that you hardly notice what is happening, unless you lose your balance.

Did you ever notice how cats always seem to land on their feet?

They do?

Butterfliers

This amazing little toy seems to defy the force of gravity. Of course, nobody can outsmart gravity. The secret is in how this toy throws its weight around. Hidden under its wings is a pair of weights that shift the center of gravity. It just defies the eyes and seems to hang in midair. Make one to sit on your desk or on your nose or to amaze someone who doesn't know the secret.

You Will Need
a small ball of clay
a stick
lightweight cardboard
two pennies
scissors
markers
tape
glue

1. Trace the butterfly onto a piece of white paper.

2. Glue it to the cardboard.

3. Cut it out as carefully as you can. Even little variations will throw it off balance.

4. Color it.

5. Make the stand by rolling up a ball of clay. Poke the stick upright in the center of the clay.

6. Just for fun, find and mark the place you predict will be the center of gravity.

7. Stick the pennyweights under the wing tips. Thick rubber cement is best.

8. Balance the butterflier on your finger. Wiggle the pennies around to make it fly straight.

9. Set it on the stand. (Now where is the center of gravity?)

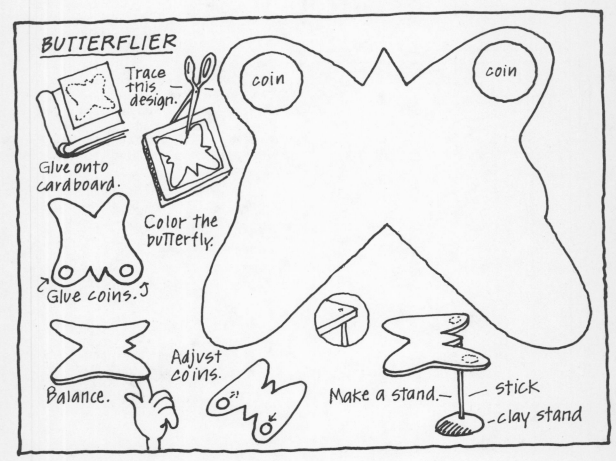

BUTTERFLIER

Trace this design.

Glue onto cardboard.

Color the butterfly.

Glue coins.

coin   coin

Balance.

Adjust coins.

Make a stand. — stick

— clay stand

112

Metamorphosis

Redesign your butterflier to be a totally different shape. Turn it into a starship or a person.

Your job is to figure out where to put the counterweights to get these contraptions to balance. The magic gravity-defying power of the butterflier comes from the fact that the center of gravity is not where it seems. Your experience tells you it's someplace in the middle. Those hidden weights (extra bits of mass) shift it. The eyes are fooled.

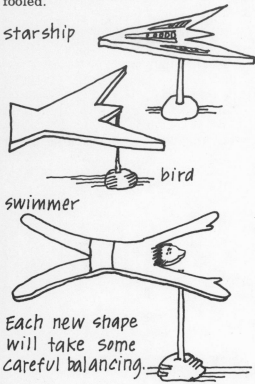

starship

bird

swimmer

Each new shape will take some careful balancing.

Outside Question

The center of mass is in the center of the mass of an object. This is *always* true. But sometimes it can exist outside an object. Impossible?

Imagine a donut. Now try to imagine where the center of mass is. It's a nice regular shape, so you should have no problem.

When you remove a dinosaur's tail, what do you have left?

Tyrannosaurus wrecks.

Animal Tails

All creatures that move on land have the problem of keeping their balance so that they don't fall and break. Running, jumping, and making quick changes in direction are all tricky balancing acts. Many animals have a piece of equipment to help them in the fine act of balancing. It is called a tail.

Watch a cat in action and you'll see that its tail is not something that is simply dragged along behind. The tail takes different shapes and positions. The cat throws the weight of its tail around to help balance its movements.

A look around the animal kingdom will show you that many animal bodies are balanced by large tails. The tails work as weights to balance animals when they move. Scientists refer to the tails as counterbalances.

Tails are not the only things that act as counterbalances. The heavy antlers of the moose, the tusks of the elephant, the large curving horns of the mountain sheep all act as counterbalances. They are all carefully designed into the animal's body plan to help it keep its balance. Of course, cats can do without tails. It might be interesting to study whether manx (tailless) cats move as easily as tailed cats. You can be sure that animals like the kangaroo would be in terrible trouble if they lost their tails.

Cone Creature

Have you ever tried to balance an ice cream cone on your nose?

You could if you could give it a tail. (You could balance a lot of things if you gave them tails.) Here is an experiment to prove the point. Stand a cone on its tip, with the help of a tail.

You Will Need
a paper cone (like the kind snow cones come in) or a sheet of paper

lightweight cardboard
two pennies
glue
tape
scissors

1. If you can't find a cone you can make one from a sheet of paper. Cut out a circle. Fold it and tape it closed (see illustrations).

2. Cut out the "tail" from a piece of cardboard.

3. Cut two 1½-inch slits on either side of the cone's tip. It will be easier if you flatten the cone to do this.

4. Slide the tail through the slits.

5. Tape the penny weights on the bottom of the tail.

6. Balance the tip on your finger. Try putting the tail in different positions. What happens to the cone? Can you balance it without a tail? With a tail but without the penny weights? Can you account for this weighty behavior?

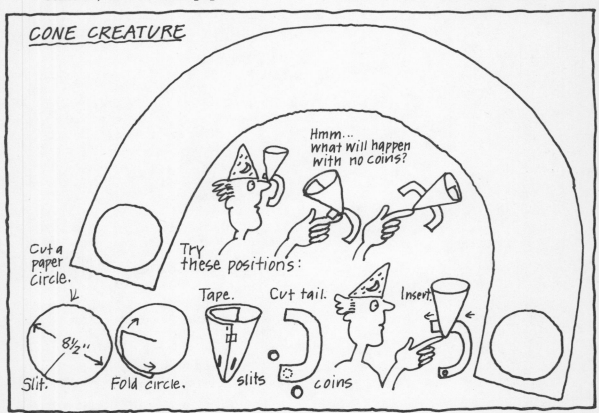

CONE CREATURE

Cut a paper circle.

8½"

Slit.

Fold circle.

Try these positions:

Hmm... what will happen with no coins?

Tape.

Cut tail.

slits

coins

Insert.

Coming up next:

May the Force Be with You: kinetics and bodies in motion

Dominoes Unleashed

A bunch of dominoes quietly standing around may not seem very energetic. They have a lot of what scientists call *potential energy*.

Give them a push and all that potential energy is unleashed and changed into *kinetic* (kin *et* ick) *energy*. This is the energy of mass in motion. Kinetic means moving.

Standing dominoes are not the only place you'll find potential energy. If you look around, you'll see it's hard not to find potential energy. Rocks on cliffs, cars parked on hills, an egg on a sloping table, a piece of wood ready to burn, gas in an engine, a water bomb waiting to be dropped—all have potential energy. You can think of potential energy as an action waiting to happen.

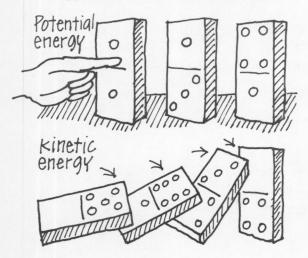

Dominoes

You've seen it on TV, in movies, and now you can have one in your very own home. It's a fantastic falling kinetic domino sculpture. Perhaps you have built one before. What you may not have known is that this sculpture has the power to transform potential energy to kinetic energy, right before your very eyes.

You Will Need
dominoes
a flat surface

1. The basic method is easy. Set each domino so that it stands up on its end. Do this on a flat surface.
2. Space each domino so that when it falls, the force of each domino topples the next domino into the next, and the next, all the way along the line. How long the process takes depends on how far apart the dominoes are spaced and on the number of dominoes you have. The more the better.

You might set up a domino sculpture with the help (and dominoes) of a friend. You can increase your domino supply at garage sales, flea markets, and junk stores.

That's just the basics. A real kinetic domino sculptor would never settle for anything so simple. Falling dominoes can be made to climb ramps, dive into water, pop balloons, change direction. All sorts of wonderful things. Check the chart for some of the possibilities. Then invent some of your own.

Energy

Energy is funny stuff. Scientists define it as the capacity to move mass or do work. You cannot make it. And you can't destroy it. But you can change it from one form to another. And you can move it around. A line of falling dominoes is a good example of energy mov-

116

DOMINOES UNLEASHED

Basic set-up.

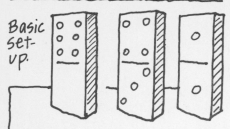

Push. →

DOMINO STUNTS

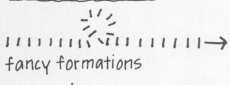

fancy formations

change in direction

DIVING DOMINO

SLIDE

strip of cardboard

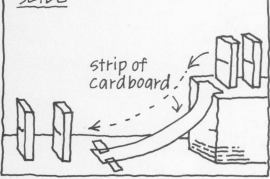

SWING

string   wire stand

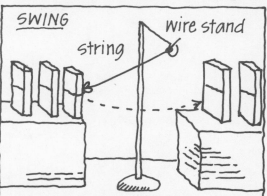

CATCH MISTAKES

Oops, mistake!

Catch it here before they all fall.

POPPER

Tape to hold.

ing from one place to another. A force (your pushy finger) topples the first domino. The force of the falling domino topples the next and the next on down the line. Besides converting all potential energy to kinetic energy, a transfer of energy has happened.

Timber!

The all-time record for the longest, most complicated feat of domino toppling belongs to the American team of John Wickham and Evez Klein. They set up 255,389 dominoes in a Japanese gymnasium in August 1980. The fall took five weeks to set up and 53 minutes to come down. The colored dominoes fell in long multiple rows, concentric circles and all sorts of complicated geometric patterns. The falling dominoes ran up ramps, released rockets, and rolled eggs into hot frying pans. It was so spectacular it appeared on Japanese TV and a photo of it in full color appears on the back cover of the *1982 Guinness Book of World Records*.

Resisting Outside Forces

Stability is a measure of how well a system resists disturbances from outside forces. How good it is at staying the way it is.

A person watching TV could be called a stable system (at least for a while). His little brother comes along and wants to force him to play. The scientific word for this kind of outside aggravation is *perturbation* (purr tur *bay* shun). Frank, the guy watching TV, resists. He resists (remains stable) until he is so perturbed that he gets upset. You might say that he becomes unstable.

In a balanced system (when some massive thing is balanced), all the forces cancel each other out. The thing is steady. Give it a nudge (a little outside force) and you will change the way the mass is distributed and the way the forces are distributed. Now gravity will tug on it a little differently. It moves. If the system is stable, the disturbance gets smaller and smaller and eventually disappears. If it is unstable, the movement will get bigger and bigger until the thing topples over and falls into a new, more stable position.

A stable situation...

becoming...

perturbed.

Gravity, An Attractive Force

All matter attracts other matter. This attraction is called gravitational force. The matter of earth pulls, or attracts. However, the earth's attraction is so large compared to an apple's attraction that the apple is almost cancelled out (but not quite). So when the stem of an apple on a tree breaks, the forces holding the stem in place are eliminated. The earth pulls the apple toward it. Although the apple pulls back, it is overwhelmed, and it falls to earth.

Weight is a measure of how strongly something is being attracted by the earth. Big masses (more matter) are more strongly attracted towards earth. We say they "weigh" more. If you ever tried to carry a bag of cement, you know it takes a lot of force in the form of muscle power to resist all the attractive forces of gravity.

This is sure an attractive mass of stuff.

Arms provide the force that keeps matter from being pulled to the earth.

Physics of Falling

Every once in a while you make a mistake and you lose your balance. Somehow the balance computer in your brain miscalculates, or works too slowly, or some unexpected force over-comes you. Your support point gets knocked out of line from your center of gravity. Or your mass suddenly arranges itself badly, with more of it on one side of your center than the other.

You are in trouble because gravity does not give up. It is constantly attracting you earthward. Your mass is going to rearrange itself to a more stable position.

Crash.

You fall.

center of gravity

When mass moves off center...

you fall.

Galileo: Fall of Authority

Kerthunk. Two thousand years of scientific "knowledge" bit the dust in a single crash. The man behind the fatal fall was Galileo, an Italian math professor. He had been experimenting with falling bodies. According to the books of the time (which was 1588) things fell at a rate proportional to their weight. That's what Aristotle had said. The heavier things were supposed to fall faster.

Galileo had other ideas. According to the story, he tested his idea by lugging an iron cannon ball and a wooden ball of an equal size (but less weight) up the Leaning Tower of Pisa. He dropped both of them at the same time. They hit smack in the middle of the town square, striking the ground at the same instant.

It was a momentous instant.

It proved that bodies fall at the same rate no matter what they weigh. It also proved that the books written by the philosophers in ancient Greek times were sometimes wrong. It also made the other professors at the university (who believed the books) look a little silly. You can imagine their amazement and their dismay. Nobody likes to find out they have been believing nonsense for 2,000 years. Galileo might have been right, but he was no hero.

The embarrassed authorities made it clear that troublemakers of his type might look for work elsewhere. He found a new job, but it didn't do any good. Galileo was in trouble with the authorities more or less for the rest of his life. The scholars of the time believed that the Greeks, who lived 2,000 years before, had pretty much figured out the universe. If you had a question you checked the books written by the ancients. Galileo's method was quite different. He looked for the answer by observing what happened in nature. He made experiments. This made the authorities uncomfortable. No wonder. He often got results that contradicted them. To make matters worse, he seemed to take special delight in making those who held the old views look silly. They did their best to ignore him, but he wouldn't keep quiet.

The worst came when he made a telescope. It had been invented in Hol-

land. When he got news of it, he experimented with tubes and lenses for a few days until he had made one himself. With it he saw that the moon had "chasms" or craters, that the sun had spots, that Jupiter had moons.

It was a sensation. Influential people from miles around came to see these impossible things through his telescope.

His reputation grew larger. He was on thin ice again, this time with the powerful church authorities. They didn't like the idea that the sun (which everyone could see that God created to be perfect) sported spots.

Jupiter's moons were especially offensive. The idea that heavenly bodies might circle a planet other than Earth directly contradicted what all the books and holy men knew to be true. Earth was said to be the immovable center of the heavens. To believe otherwise was forbidden. After all, who but the church should know more about heaven? To challenge this was too much. Galileo was told that only a heretic (a faithless, godless person) would think otherwise. It was made clear that he ought to change his views. He didn't. Late in his life he published a paper stating the truth as he saw it with his telescope. He was brought to trial and was found guilty as an enemy of the church. He was given the choice of signing a paper that said he was mistaken about what he had written or facing horrible torture.

Galileo signed and lived the rest of his life under house arrest. However, Galileo's inquiring spirit was not arrested. He is given credit for discovering the laws of force and motion and for starting the science of astronomy. His really big contribution was his way of finding out about the world, by observing and experimenting with it directly. His method continues to this day. It is called the scientific method.

I can hardly wait for the brick test.

Flight of the Feather Bomb

What falls faster, a pound of feathers or a pound of bricks? Ask ten people and see how many different answers you get.

It's a simple question. But it seems to cause a lot of confusion. It is probably the same question that got Aristotle confused. He was a famous natural philosopher who thought that an object falls with a speed that depended on its weight. People agreed with him for 2,000 years.

A feather falls slower than a brick, no doubt about it.

As it falls, it is falling through air. We tend to forget about air, rather like a fish probably forgets about water, because we don't see it. When something falls, it is pushing air molecules aside. A heavy body does this pushy job better than a lightweight body, especially if the light body has a lot of surface area that needs to push through the air. So the answer to the question of which falls faster, a pound of feathers or a pound of bricks, is—it depends. If you can squash up a pound of feathers to a small enough size (volume), it will fall at the same speed as a pound of bricks. If the feathers fall all spread out, they will fall more slowly. That's because they have a harder time pushing the air aside.

Falling, Flying, Gliding

The shape of things makes a big difference in how they get around and whether or not they can get off the ground. The study of how things push air around, and how air pushes them back, is called *aerodynamics* (air motions).

Man's study of how things fly is an ancient one, even though we have only recently been able to get off the ground ourselves. One of the best flight designers in the business is Mother Nature. You can look at almost any manmade invention for flying and find its equal in nature. You might want to make your own study of flying things (aerodynamics). It is a fascinating subject.

PREDICT HOW THESE THINGS WILL FLY, THEN TEST...

I predict a quick straight flight of a water balloon.

seeds

helicopter

paper plane

dollar bill

crumpled paper

seed pods

spiderling

skinny and fat leaves

Feathers are designed to create air resistance.

Splat Testing

Like Galileo you might want to put some of these theories to the test. Paint drops are a good way to experiment with the force of falling. Plus you get some colorful results. Before you begin sending drops crashing to the floor, predict how the splats will change as they fall farther and farther.

You Will Need
washable ink or paint
an eyedropper
paper (big sheets)
a yardstick
tape
newspaper

1. This project can be messy, so to be safe, do it outdoors or cover the area with a layer of newspaper.

2. Tape down a sheet of paper so it lies tight against the floor.

3. The paint should be thin, more like ink than paint for the best splats.

4. Before you start testing, practice a bit so you can squeeze out one drop at a time.

5. Start by dropping the paint from a distance of 1 inch.

6. Let the next drop fall from a distance of 6 inches.

7. Let the next drop fall from a distance of 12 inches.

8. Continue adding 6-inch intervals to the fall until you run out of yardstick.

Does the paint continue to break apart more and more explosively? Or is there a limit to how much you can force a drop to break apart? Are there forces in the paint that resist the force of impact? What might they be?

Just for a little splat fun you might try dropping two different colors, one on top of the other for some mixed results. Try dropping thicker paint and compare the splats.

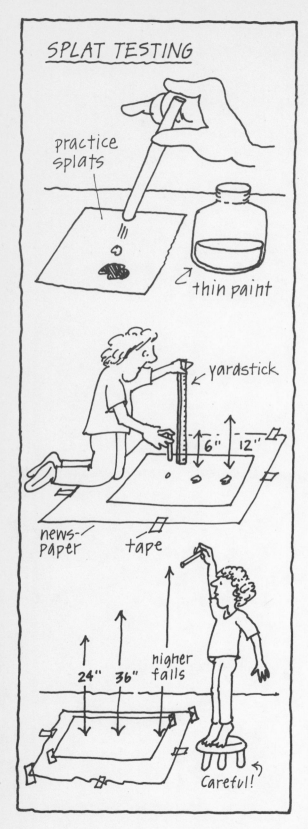

SPLAT TESTING

practice splats

thin paint

yardstick

6" 12"

newspaper

tape

24" 36" higher falls

Careful!

Splat Reading

Can you guess which of these splats fell the farthest? Don't guess. Use their shapes to help you put them in order. Then check your results in the back of the book.

One way that scientists know that their experiments are working is that other scientists check their results. The other scientists try the experiments themselves. If they get the same results, they can be fairly sure that the conclusions are right. If they don't, then there is a good chance something is funny. Perhaps a freak accident. Or the theory was screwy. Or they didn't do exactly what they thought they did. Check your splats against these and see if your results check out.

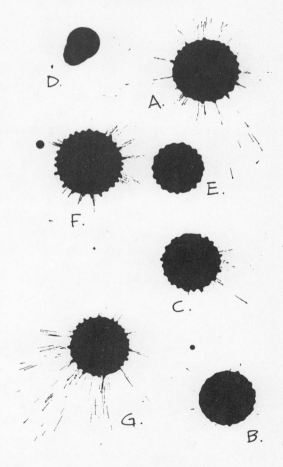

D.

A.

F.

E.

C.

G.

B.

Marble Run

It's best not to throw yourself off some high place to investigate falling. But you can do something else. A marble falling down ramps is perfect for the job. The challenge is to invent ways to keep the marble falling down a series of ramps but to make the trip take as long as possible. Use friction to slow the fall.

You Will Need
a scrap of plywood
strips of wood
a marble
white glue
miscellaneous items, such as pill
  bottles, rubber bands, nails, plastic
  caps, plastic strips

1. Prop the board so it leans back at an angle.

2. Put glue on one side of the strips. Stick a strip onto the board at an angle so the marble will roll downward. (Remember: adjust the slope so the marble will roll *slowly*.)

3. Glue on another strip that slopes in the opposite direction. Make sure to leave enough room so that the marble can drop down to the next level.

4. Put in a stop if the marble is rolling too fast to drop down to the next level.

5. Now put your inventor's cap on and think of ways to create friction that will slow the fall.

The object is to get the marble to run as long a time as possible, without stopping. The illustrations give you some ideas how this might be accomplished.

Friction

Chuck a stone off a cliff and it soon hits the bottom. Roll the same stone off the same cliff and it takes a lot longer to get to the same spot at the bottom. It had to bump and thump its way down. All that rubbing resistance (friction) slowed it down.

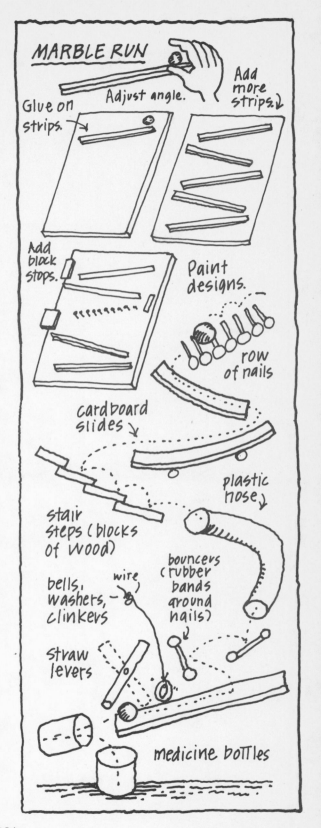

MARBLE RUN

Glue on strips.

Adjust angle.

Add more strips.

Add block stops.

Paint designs.

row of nails

cardboard slides

plastic nose

stair steps (blocks of wood)

bouncers (rubber bands around nails)

bells, washers, clinkers

wire

straw levers

medicine bottles

Coming up next:

The Back of the Book: answers you've been waiting for

Answer to page 21

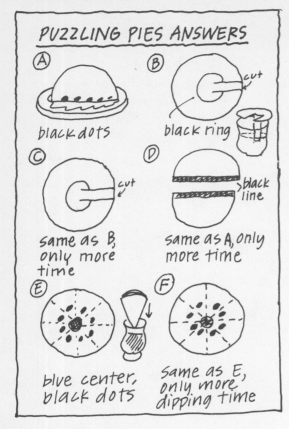

PUZZLING PIES ANSWERS

Ⓐ black dots

Ⓑ black ring `cut`

Ⓒ `cut` same as B, only more time

Ⓓ black line same as A, only more time

Ⓔ blue center, black dots

Ⓕ Same as E, only more dipping time

Answer to page 30

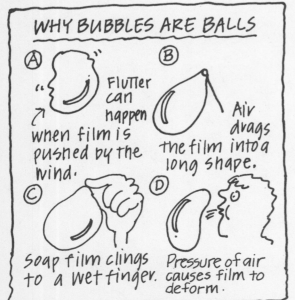

WHY BUBBLES ARE BALLS

Ⓐ Flutter can happen when film is pushed by the wind.

Ⓑ Air drags the film into a long shape.

Ⓒ Soap film clings to a wet finger.

Ⓓ Pressure of air causes film to deform.

Answer to page 43

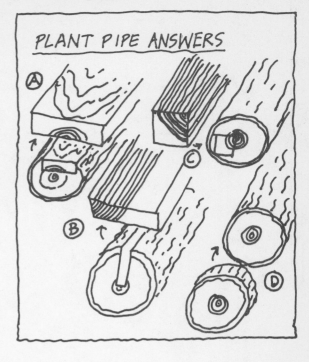

PLANT PIPE ANSWERS

Ⓐ Ⓑ Ⓒ Ⓓ

Answer to page 54

INSOLUBLE ANSWER

To get the oil, tip and pour off the oil layer.

oil
water

To get the water out, invert the bottle, tip and pour out the water.

water

Answer to page 56

FAT TRAP
(one possible solution)

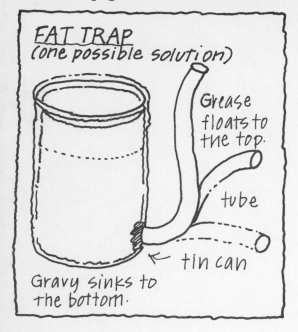

Grease floats to the top.

tube

← tin can

Gravy sinks to the bottom.

Answer to page 123

SPLAT ANSWERS

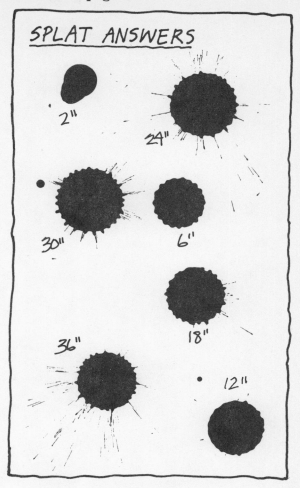

2"

24"

30"

6"

36"

18"

12"

Answer to page 59

FLOATING ANSWER

Pour alcohol in the jar first. Because it is lighter, it will float to the top through the heavier water, mixing as it goes.

For an Absorbing Answer, turn to the next page.

Answer to page 93

SYMMETRICAL OR NOT?

The asymmetrical items include hand, key, the shells, scissors, paper clip, duck (from the side-view point).

ABSORBING ANSWER

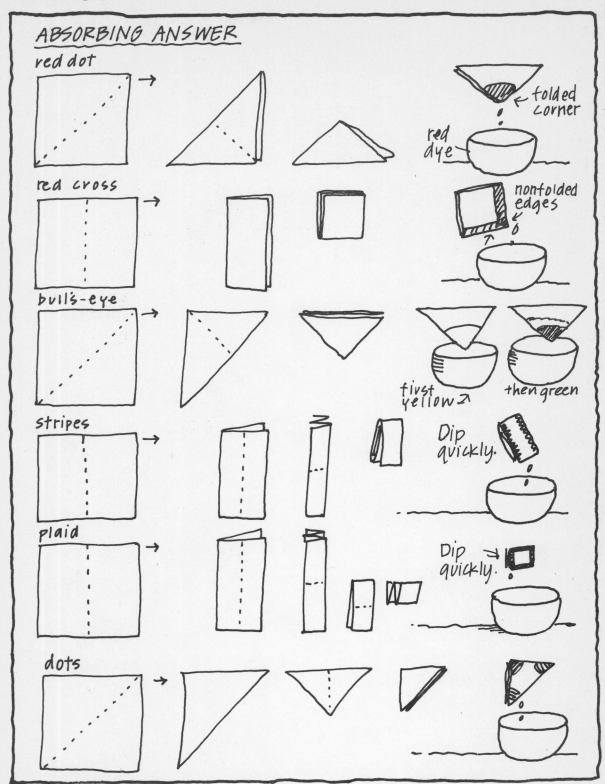

red dot

folded corner

red dye

red cross

nonfolded edges

bull's-eye

first yellow

then green

stripes

Dip quickly.

plaid

Dip quickly.

dots